KEN TYRRELL

Other books by this author:

Michael Schumacher
The greatest of all?

Inside the Mind of the Grand Prix driver
The psychology of the fastest men on earth: sex,
danger and everything else

Murray Walker (paperback)
The *very* last word

Murray Walker (hardback)
The last word

The motorsport art of Juan Carlos Ferrigno

Hitler's Grands Prix in England
Donington 1937 and 1938

Ayrton Senna
As time goes by

Ayrton Senna
The legend grows

Ayrton Senna
His full car racing record

KEN TYRRELL

PORTRAIT OF A MOTOR RACING GIANT

CHRISTOPHER HILTON

First published in July 2002

A catalogue record for this book is available from the
British Library

ISBN 1 85960 885 X

Library of Congress catalog card no. 2002103349

Published by Haynes Publishing, Sparkford,
Yeovil, Somerset BA22 7JJ, UK.

Tel: 01963 442030 Fax 01963 440001
Int. tel: +44 1963 442030 Int. fax: +44 1963 440001
E-mail: sales@haynes-manuals.co.uk
Website: www.haynes.co.uk

Haynes North America Inc.,
861 Lawrence Drive, Newbury Park,
California 91320, USA.

Designed by Simon Larkin
Page layout by Chris Fayers, Morwenstow, Cornwall
Printed and bound in England by
J. H. Haynes & Co. Ltd, Sparkford

CONTENTS

PROLOGUE

'It was a race at Albi [France] in 1967. Ken was moaning because the Union Jack was upside down.'

Keith Boshier

The last time, the face was gaunt but the eyes still danced with delight and the laughter still began as a giggle and rose through a gurgle to a great, glorious guffawing. If he was unduly excited, or arguing, or telling somebody off the guffaw became what everybody refers to as 'a froth job'. He frothed all over you. In fact, Bert Baldwin – a Goodyear tyre technician who worked with the team – insists that 'he often actually did foam at the mouth, did Ken'.

Mark Stewart, son of Sir Jackie, puts it neatly enough. 'I've seen what a froth job looks like, the Ken Tyrrell froth job when he's telling you off. If you haven't had one of those, you haven't lived.'

Spring 2001, and we're sitting in the corner of a pub called The Barley Mow, a mile or two from where, on 3 May 1924, Ken Tyrrell was born. At one level the location has no particular relevance because Tyrrell lived and worked hereabouts for most of his life, but at another level The Barley Mow is almost exquisitely appropriate: a very English place where you're always thinking you'll bang your head against the beams, and the clientele are old enough to talk, quite naturally, about pre-war cricket. The restaurant, across the stone flag floor from the bar, has an extensive menu but somehow, around our table of six, the bangers and mash seems right.

On one side of the table sit Tyrrell, his son Bob who has driven him here, and Mark Stewart, a talented documentary maker who is doing some filming of Tyrrell.

When I'd rung Tyrrell to arrange the lunch he'd said: 'Don't think I can make it that day, Mark's coming.'

Days of pomp and circumstance: Jackie Stewart wins the 1973 Austrian Grand Prix from his Tyrrell team-mate François Cevert (Schlegelmilch).

I said: 'Bring him along.'

'OK!'

It was frequently so. Throughout his life he spoke a great deal but he never wasted words, especially on the telephone. Several of his drivers will be testifying to that.

On our side of the table sit Eoin Young, a journalist measuring his career to the 1960s and for whom motor racing and bangers and mash might have been invented; Nigel Roebuck, a journalist covering Formula 1 with distinction since the 1970s, and myself.

Please remember that like many people long involved in Formula 1, Tyrrell had travelled on an immense scale although this in no way softened his Englishness. He spoke to foreigners loudly and always in English. Jackie Stewart judges that if he had ever said a word in French it would likely have been a naughty one – but he probably didn't.

Please remember, too, that a non-travelling member of his team – Keith Boshier – was deputed to go to the factory on the Sunday night of any victory anywhere in the world and hoist the Union Jack up the flagpole.

The rock upon which all was built, Ken and Norah. She survived him by a few months. (Schlegelmilch).

'It was a race at Albi [France] in 1967,' Boshier explains. 'Ken was moaning because the Union Jack was upside down. After the race we'd got a bit too much to drink I suppose, climbed up and took the Union Jack down – and we took the Belgian flag because we had Jacky Ickx driving for us then. That Union Jack stayed up in the old wooden shed at the factory for years and years. Then we used it for victory hoisting and when we finally moved the race cars out of the old shed I brought it home. It's been up in the loft ever since.'

Yes, the bangers and mash seemed right. Tyrrell sipped a half pint of Guinness.

The talk, as it invariably did with Ken Tyrrell, moved along easily – punctuated by the giggle-gurgle-guffaws – and ranged evenly over matters arising. Although motorsport was always at the core, Tyrrell did not restrict himself to that – he could have joined the old hands at the bar discussing the cricket of the 1930s quite naturally, for example – but his particular common sense seemed applicable to everything. He was known in motorsport as

Uncle Ken for this wisdom as much as for the paternalistic connotations of that phrase. If you were talking nonsense he told you so in an amiable, schoolmasterish sort of way, and guffawed afterwards, but you knew you'd been told and, curiously, liked him more for it. One time I'd been talking about a South American goalkeeper in the World Cup. He craned that craggy head towards me and said: 'You're talking balls.' Then he explained why . . .

(Another time, he was showing me round the factory at Ockham, a few minutes drive from The Barley Mow, and we came into the design office where a large drawing stretched across a board. It was so detailed and complicated it might have been anything, especially to a non-technician like me.

'Cover it up!' he ordered the draughtsman.

'Listen,' I said, 'I wouldn't even know if it was upside down – and you know I wouldn't.'

'Makes no difference. Cover it up!'

And we both stood there laughing like children, no schoolmaster in sight, while the draughtsman discreetly laid sheets of white paper over it.)

If you take six people who are by nature good company then an hour is a moment, and the memories get richer and more improbable and all the better for that; and never did Ken Tyrrell admonish anyone by saying you were outsiders listening at the door; I was inside. He used memory and judgement because he had both but he never flaunted anything, especially the view from the inside, to make a point or trump anyone in an argument.

The big feller was far, far too big for that.

Just once during the lunch the talk fell to aeroplane travel and I recounted a tale Kenneth Tyrrell, his eldest son and a British Airways pilot, had related to me of how he was doing the London-Edinburgh shuttle and, coming back, the plane was struck by lightning. A passenger became so hysterical that Kenneth was called to calm her, which he did by explaining that lightning had no great effect on planes. 'Well,' she demanded to know, 'when was the last time you were on one when it happened?' In that deep, diplomatic voice which Ken, Kenneth and Bob could all summon when required, he murmured: 'On the way up . . .'

Tyrrell adored that anecdote and took up the running

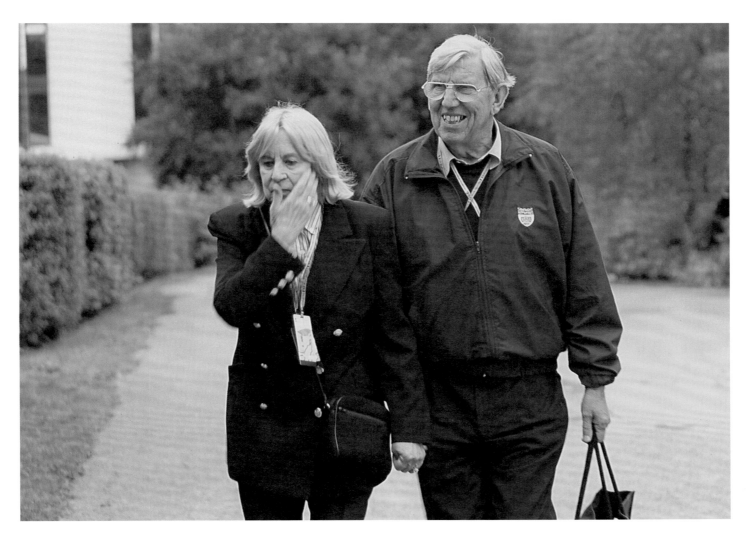

but in a subtly different way. 'We were travelling back from the Australian Grand Prix on a Jumbo,' he said, 'and as the plane was going along a voice came on the tannoy. "This is your captain speaking. We are now cruising at X altitude and doing Y speed." Pause. "Happy birthday, mum!"'

Kenneth was flying it, and this was the birthday of Ken's beloved wife Norah.

This memory was so strong – pride in his son, pride in his family – that he turned away, tears welling in his eyes; caught that quickly and turned back, guffawing. We knew he was ill, we didn't know how bad it was, but for him to get so close to breaking down betrayed something about what the illness was doing to him. I had seen him look away like this once before – but we'll be coming to that soon enough.

The lunch completed, I needed a mini-interview and we went to a side room where the rise and fall of conversation from the bar wouldn't interfere with my tape recorder, and, as we prepared to begin, the juke box at our elbow suddenly exploded in sound, AꓭBA pumping 'Money-money-money' round us and through us.

The Tyrrell-Stewart family closeness (above) spanned generations (Phipps/Sutton). The Tyrrell team spanned the generations (opposite). This is Mark Blundell at Jerez in 1994 with the Ferrari of Jean Alesi – who'd made his début in a Tyrrell – tucked in behind (Sutton).

We retreated to the people-carrier Bob had driven him here in. He moved cleanly and professionally through the questions and answers, always thoughtful, answering in lovely summaries of situations, although at one point I asked: 'What about Bernie Ecclestone's part?'

'You know I'm not going to talk about that,' he said, the schoolmaster again.

The interview concluded, Bob drove him off and he was waving as he went, that gaunt face wreathed in a smile behind the window.

'I'm glad we had that lunch,' Roebuck said. 'You never know.'

I think I did.

I think Roebuck did, too. He was slightly reassured that Tyrrell had sipped his way through the half pint but, reflecting, said: 'Although Ken wasn't a big drinker he adored Guinness and ordinarily would have had a couple of pints.'

We never saw him again.

A curiosity is that, although Tyrrell was happy enough to give interviews and talk about anything you wanted (except sometimes Ecclestone) he had absolutely no interest in co-operating in a book about his life. A succession of hopefuls (me included) journeyed to his door and tried to persuade him that his story should necessarily be told. He rebuffed us all in various ways – mine took the form of 'nobody ever tells the truth in books, so why bother?' What he meant was that the politics and deals within Formula 1 over the years, at which the imagination shudders, always remain in their secret places. Too many are implicated, the places are too sensitive. I tried to explain that nobody really cares about that, or rather the few who do read the financial, not the sports, pages. He looked at me in that way which said 'never going to change my mind,' let that settle and then guffawed.

The story is about men and machines, the money relegated to its true role of facilitating – nothing more.

Cumulatively, however, Tyrrell did talk a great deal and

those embraced by his career are invariably talkers, too. And there was plenty to talk about most days for going on five decades. I am particularly grateful to his son Bob (who has inherited the Tyrrell openness) for charting the family background as well as throwing light on Formula 1 matters.

Duncan Rabagliati combed his records with astonishing diligence (and willingness) to recreate as far as possible Tyrrell's own driving career, something which I don't think has ever been done before. Martin Hadwen of the Motor Racing Archive combed his records, too. (If you want to see the treasure trove there, or indeed want to contribute material to it, visit http://www.motorracing-archive.com.)

For permission to quote, I sincerely thank Renaud de Laborderie (*François Cevert*/Solar, 1973); José Rosinski (*Depailler: La Course est un Combat*/Calmann-Lévy, 1978).

Nigel Roebuck lent a long interview he did with Derek Gardner on the six-wheel Tyrrell and I am grateful to Gardner himself for expanding on certain points, answering criticism and providing background. Mark Stewart gave a frank interview and allowed me to use extracts from his

moving documentary *Ken Tyrrell: Surviving Formula 1* (Duke). Sir Jackie gave a frank interview, too and thanks to Jean Albrecht, his secretary, for her organisational skills. Chris Knapman and John Briscoe of Collectors Carbooks dug out precious old *Autosports* and race books instantly.

Many other people gave of their time and their memories: ex-Tyrrell employees Neil Davis, Keith Boshier and Chris Leslie; Julian Bailey, Jean-Pierre Jarier, Derek Daly, Mark Blundell, ex-Goodyear personnel Barrie Griffin, Graham Ball and Bert Baldwin; Martin Streeton, Barrie Barker of Ockham Football Club, Charles Hewett, Danny Sullivan, Alan Brown, Jean-Pierre Beltoise, Martyn Pass of Audi UK, Eoin Young for particular help and kindnesses, Jean Alesi, Brian Henton, Ricardo Rosset, Jody Scheckter, Johnny Servoz-Gavin, Jacky Ickx and Jonathan Palmer.

Simon Taylor, chairman of Haymarket Magazines Ltd, and David Prasher, publisher, gave permission to quote from *Autosport*, something particularly important because their coverage reaches right back into Tyrrell's career as a driver. Those distant fragments are precious to the whole story.

Chapter One

CHOPPER

*'Dad took the last cake away. My brother asked "Why?"
and dad said: "because you've got a friend coming. He'll
want one, too, won't he?" So he showed us how to behave.'*

Bob Tyrrell

*'He was not a robust footballer but he was forthright. Not
particularly fast, a typical centre-half. He was made for the
job.'*

Charles Hewlett

*'I am not an engineer and I feel I am totally incapable of
conceiving a racing car. I am not a businessman – which I
regret.'*

Ken Tyrrell

The past was not just another country to Ken Tyrrell, it
was an uninteresting place. He'd look back if you asked
him to, but he lived entirely in the present and for the future.
The idea of dwelling on – and in – the great days was remote
from him. There is a concensus of opinion that, however
absurd the notion seems, he was genuinely unaware of the
scale of his achievements. He remained a young man all his
life, charged and sustained by great enthusiasms. He
delighted in being alive.

He was born at West Horsley near a pub called The Duke
of Wellington. Perhaps that explains the love of Guinness.
West Horsley is now one of those villages which have grown
into a place of wealth and style – there's a railway station
and the line leads directly to London and the big money
which, nightly, the commuters bring back. The villages
around reflect that, too: East Horsley and Ockham. This is
the gentle countryside of the Home Counties, verdant and
often manicured.

*Urging his Cooper, one-handed, round Snetterton in 1953 – to
fifth place (Guy Griffiths).*

13

The family background is by no means complete. Tyrrell's youngest son, Bob, says that 'dad was born 3 May 1924. He had a half brother, Bert. Dad's father, who was a gamekeeper, married two or three times. I can't remember if dad's mum was his second or his third wife. So Bert had the same father but not the same mother. There was a sister called Irene who lived up in Yorkshire.'

Young Tyrrell 'wanted to go to technical college,' as he said himself, 'but I failed the entrance exam, then I sat my 11-Plus and I failed that as well. And then I tried to get into the RAF as a boy entrant but I failed the entrance exam. Then I got lucky because the war broke out and the RAF would take anyone. I became a flight engineer which meant I flew in the latter part of the war.'[1] It seems that he did not see active service. Bob insists that 'he forged his birth certificate to get in because he had left school when he was 14 and it was now coming up towards the end of the war.'

During these RAF days he found himself in Edinburgh – he was 18 or 19 – and met a blonde beauty. He proposed to her almost immediately by telegram and she accepted. She was called Norah.

Paul Tear, a close friend, said this at Tyrrell's memorial service: 'After forging his application – well probably mis-stating the details on his birth-certificate is a nicer way of putting it – Ken was accepted into the RAF during the war as a trainee flight engineer, despite being under age. He was posted to Scotland for his training, and it was here – at the Palais de Dance in Edinburgh, to be exact – that he met the wee Scottish flower, and love of his life, Norah. Three months later, with money borrowed for the licence, they got married.'

In the late 1990s, Tyrrell would say: 'for the last 55 years I've been waking up every morning with a beautiful naked woman lying beside me.'

One of the men who drove for him, Jean Alesi, would say that he had never met two people more suited to spending their lives together. They married in 1943 and their first son, Kenneth, was born in 1944.

Bert had set up a timber business at Ockham, in a former brick works. Bert evidently did not serve in the war because timber – like farming, for example – was called a reserved occupation: important enough to the war effort that you stayed in it.

When Tyrrell was demobbed he got '£25 and a new suit for five and a half years' service. I set out to make my own way in life.' Bob adds to that: 'What I do know is that when dad left the RAF, he went to work in Leatherhead assembling lighters at Ronson's lighter factory. Then his brother invited him to join him in the timber business, and he never looked back.'

Of this timber business, Tyrrell said: 'To begin with, we were mostly topping and lopping off trees. After about two years, we bought a lorry for transporting other people's trees. Once or twice we had trees to sell, and this seemed to be more profitable so we became buyers and sellers.'

Bob was born in 1949 and by then Tyrrell had resumed an enthusiasm which had held him since childhood: football. He joined Ockham in the Tillingbourne Valley League and a man who was in the same team, Charles Hewlett, gives the background. 'Like many others I came out of the Forces in 1946 – I was three or four years older than Ken. Some of us had married local girls and others were Ockham chaps anyway. We reformed the football club, which had been closed down during the war. In fact, the ground had been ploughed up for farming. The pavilion was a wooden shed, that's all. It had a cold water standpipe outside. We changed in the shed or went home on our bikes and changed there – not many of us had baths in those days. It was all a bit primitive, but we enjoyed it.'

Now it was around 1949. 'He lived in Horsley and he came and joined us. It's as simple as that, really.' The timber business was situated approximately mid-way between Horsley and Ockham.

'He was not a robust footballer but he was forthright,' Hewlett says. 'Not particularly fast, a typical centre-half. He was made for the job. He didn't shout a lot and he scored the odd goal. The whole atmosphere was very friendly between teams – there was none of this over-the-top tackling or that sort of thing. You just went for the ball, did your best and had a good game. We did play one particular game against Horsley, which is much bigger than Ockham and they normally played in a league slightly higher up the

The very beginning (above) – Woodcote in July 1951 and somewhere in that crowd is Ken Tyrrell, at his first motor race meeting and falling in love with it. This is the 500cc event which impressed him so much (Autosport). The end (right). Ricardo Rosset fails to qualify for the 1998 Japanese Grand Prix – Tyrrell's last race (Sutton).

scale than us. His brother Bert played right-back for
Horsley and I happened to play left wing – I'm a bit of a
miniature, a 10-stone chap. It was a very good game and
you knew you'd been playing against Bert because you had
a few bruises afterwards to prove it. Ken said at half time:
"Keep it up, Charlie, you're making him run
round in circles" – meaning his brother. It was
all good-natured banter.' (Mind you, Bob
suggests 'there were a lot of professional fouls'
and it may be from here, rather than the
timberyard, that the nickname 'Chopper' came –
but, wherever, he was known as Chopper.)

*Somehow the
setting of the
modern factory
still bore the
homely character
of the wood yard
. . . The proprietor,
1996 (Sutton).*

'We were in the final of the Tillingbourne
Valley cup. It was played at Albury, a well-
known beauty spot with a lovely football pitch,' Hewlett
says. 'We played against Holmbury St Mary, another
village, who were our great rivals for two or three seasons
and we took a coachload of supporters. Unheard of! We
lost 4-2 . . .'

In 1951, as Tyrrell would remember, the football club
'got up a coach party to go to Silverstone' to watch the
BRMs at the British Grand Prix.[2] We threw some beer in the
back of the bus and I saw my first motor race. As soon as I
saw it I fell in love with it. I'd never even read anything
about motor racing before that, but it really got to me. I
found it terribly exciting.'

He had found something else – the rest of his life.

Silverstone had, like so many circuits, been built on an
old air force base, and, like them, was rudimentary. The
crowd stood very close to the cars and unprotected except
for straw bales here and there. Tyrrell and the Ockham
coach party made their way to Stowe Corner, the fast right-
hander at the end of Hangar Straight. They'd see Froilan
Gonzalez win the Grand Prix in a Ferrari, with Reg Parnell
in the BRM fifth and five laps down but, it seems, a
supporting race – the very hectic International 500cc
category – fired Tyrrell's new enthusiasm. A driver called
Alan Brown had qualified third in a Cooper car (John

Above: The anonymity of a driving career (Autosport, August 1952). Left: The first season, 1952, exploring Silverstone's broad acres (Guy Griffiths). Below: Silverstone again, in August 1952, where Ken Tyrrell finished tenth in a heat of the Formula 3 race but didn't finish the final (Guy Griffiths).

Cooper himself was in the race) with pole going to a certain Stirling Moss. What caught Tyrrell's eye was that Brown came from Guildford – and Tyrrell had just bought his first house there. They lived about a mile apart.

Brown describes 500cc Formula 3 as 'very competitive and exciting and expensive: it wasn't just fun, it was serious.' It was also a proving ground because Tyrrell, watching so intently, had seen two men who would go on to Formula 1: Ken Wharton and Peter Collins – and Moss, of course.

On the first lap the little cars came round in a shoal, two and three abreast. During the race, *Autosport* magazine reported a driver called Don Parker 'hit a marker tin at Stowe, his car shot into the air, bounced off four other markers but stayed on its wheels.' Moss would win easily. Towards the end he 'was taking it easy now, and caused a roar of laughter by taking both hands off the wheel at Stowe and having a good look at a plane flying overhead.'

All this captivated Tyrrell. He would pop round and see Brown – sixth in the race, a couple of minutes behind Moss – when they got home.

'He knew I lived in Guildford,' Brown says, 'and I seem to remember he used to come down to the house. We had a large garage where we could prepare the cars. He'd come down and chat. That's how it started.' (Neil Davis, who would become one of Tyrrell's first motor racing employees, confirms this folklore. 'Brown lived in Guildford and the story goes that Ken knocked on his door and said: "I'd like to have a look at your car." Alan Brown obliged, and at the end of the year Ken bought it from him.')

Brown remembers calling in once at Tyrrell's house, but he wasn't in and so he chatted to Norah instead.

Norah remembers 'soon' after Silverstone Tyrrell 'got the idea of part-buying a racing car, which I wasn't keen on at all because we didn't have a great deal of cash. Don't forget Ken was still in the timber business then.'

'She probably didn't like the idea of me being away and she'd be left with two small children, but she realised it was going to be difficult to talk me out of it,' Tyrrell would say.[3]

There's mild confusion about what happened next. Brown is sure he was selling one of his racing cars and advertised it in *Autosport* – an advert which Tyrrell saw and

acted on. Tyrrell never, as far as I am aware, spoke of this advert but he certainly did speak of buying a car from Brown. He also spoke of Brown saying: 'If you can't get round Brands Hatch in under a minute you might as well forget it.' Brands was then a mile long and much favoured by the Formula 3 drivers.

'Anyway,' Brown says, 'he went ahead and bought it. Typical Ken; he said: "You didn't say about the minute until after I'd bought it!" He had a great sense of humour. Did I only tell him after I'd sold the car to him? When you're in business, you're in business and you're selling something, aren't you?'

So Ken Tyrrell embarked on his career as a driver, beginning in 1952. He took the car to Brands Hatch and did get round in under a minute, an experience he found 'frightening' but not frightening enough to put him off.

I cannot resist setting out two results to prove how comparatively modest this career would be. The *Motor Year Book* 1954, covering 1953 – Tyrrell's second season, of course – filled 226 pages with reports, reviews and results. There are only two mentions of Tyrrell, in a section which bore the heading Principal Competitions:

Charterhall National Meeting
May 23. 1 lap: 2 miles (15 laps)

1 Gerard	Cooper	76mph
2 Tyrell [sic]	Cooper	
3 Paulson	Kieft	

Silverstone 100-miles Race
August 22. Half-Litre Car Club Meeting.
Commander Yorke Trophy (100 miles, 63 laps)

1 Westcott	Cooper	1:29:4
2 Tyrell [sic]	Cooper	
3 Symonds	Cooper	

I am indebted to Duncan Rabagliati for recreating the statistics of Tyrrell's career because it enables us to see its scope, however modest. (His full career, race-by-race, is in the Statistics at the end of the book.) It began at Goodwood on 2 June 1952 when he took part in Heat 1 of the 500cc International trophy. He retired. He didn't rate a single mention in *Autosport* and no surprise about that.

Two months later at Silverstone, Tyrrell got his mention.

'Pleasantly warm weather graced the meeting, which began with two ten-lap "curtain raisers". The first, the Junior race, was won by I. L. Bueb . . . a Cooper-Norton driven by R. K. Tyrrell was second.' In the second heat of the 100 miles race that same afternoon, Tyrrell was tenth.

He drove in seven meetings in 1952 and 14 in 1953, including his first win, at Beveridge Park, on 25 April. Now *Autosport* included him in a headline:

"SCHWEPPERVESCENT" BEVERIDGE
Charles Headland (Kieft) has Mixed Fortunes in Scottish
500 c.c. Meeting—Newcomer K. Tyrrell (Cooper) does well

In Heat 3, two cars dropped out and 'this left K. Tyrrell with a fair lead.' He won it at an average of 60.2mph. He also won Heat 4 and the Final. 'In this, 500s at their best were witnessed in a really terrific duel between Headland and K. Tyrrell. It says much for Tyrrell that he managed to hold a good first lap getaway against the more experienced Headland. And Charles was definitely motoring! That Kieft went round the circuit like the hammers, so much so that Charles broke his own lap record by two clear seconds. Yet he still couldn't take Tyrrell, but I believe another hundred yards might have done it and the Cooper driver was highly delighted to see the chequered flag.'[4]

All this time he was in the timber business – a sign to the timber yard at Ockham said simply:

TYRRELL BROs LTD
TIMBER MERCHANTS
Tel: Ripley 25 25

He was also raising his family. 'We hardly ever went on holiday because in the early days there probably wasn't enough money and in the latter days you had the racing,' Bob says. 'We only had two family holidays that I remember. One was at Poole in Dorset and the other was in Majorca. I always remember him being late picking me up from school because he had so much to do.

'He was very good at teaching us things through example. For instance, one of my brother's friends was coming after lunch to join him at the house. There were a couple of cream cakes. People ate cream cakes all the time, Sunday afternoon you'd stuff yourself with them. There were cakes with whipped cream on and Kenneth was about to take the last one. Dad took the cake away. Kenneth asked "Why?" and dad said: "because you've got a friend coming. He'll want one, too, won't he?" So he showed us how to behave. It didn't matter who he was speaking to, he had as much respect for somebody who was a racing driver as somebody who did a lowly job.'

He raced in 20 meetings in 1954 and 20 again in 1955 and in August of that year achieved his most notable success [and the only one he ever referred to!]. First, he travelled to Sweden and in the Swedish Grand Prix meeting put the Cooper on the front row of the Formula 3 race. In the race he took the lead on lap 2 but a driver called Hutchy Hutchinson crashed trying to get in at the back, 'escaped with a shaking, and Tyrell's [sic] motor packed up.' The following week, *Autosport* corrected this with a paragraph in their Pit and Paddock notes. Tyrrell's retirement was not 'engine trouble' but 'owing to a fractured drive shaft, incurred when Hutchinson's Cooper struck his nearside rear wheel. Ken's engine . . . has not missed a beat this season.'

This same issue reported the success, in a 15-lap Formula 3 race at Karlskoga a week later. A Cooper driver, André Loens, 'challenged Tyrrell for the lead but after scrapping heartily for eight laps he dropped back with mechanical troubles.' Tyrrell won by 1.3 seconds.

Bob Tyrrell has a lovely anecdote and he's pretty sure it centres around Karlskoga. 'I was fishing at the time – I was a lad then and we stayed in a place on a pike lake, a big lake just full of pike in the middle of Sweden. I wasn't interested in racing, I wanted to go fishing. I was only young. I caught a pike and we had it for dinner. It must have tasted bloody awful . . .'

After winning Karlskoga, Tyrrell got a test drive for Aston Martin at Silverstone – 'I did quite well in the test, actually' in a car he felt was the best he'd ever driven, 'wonderful . . . and very fast'. The Aston people had a chat with him afterwards and said they were looking for 'a Number 6 to go in a three-car team. Stirling Moss got to be Number 1 and they no longer needed a Number 6.'

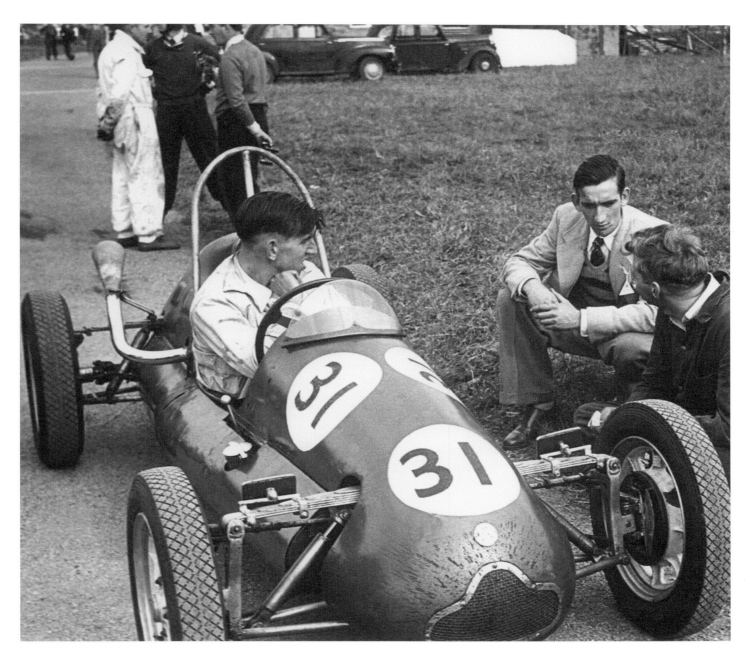

Listening in the cockpit to a conversation at Castle Combe, October 1952 – and no doubt he'd have had a thing or two to add (Guy Griffiths).

Guffaw . . .

Innocent days. A book called *The Motor Racing Directory*, covering the 1955 season, gave details of all the leading British drivers: their notable results (evidently he had been third in the 500cc Championship of Ireland) and their personal details. Tyrrell, already a member of the British Racing Driver's Club, was described as a 'forestry contractor' and his home address as Sheepfold Road, Guildford. Tel. 2512.

As the years moved by, Tyrrell began to lose pleasure in driving because he realised he wasn't getting anywhere. In 1956 he raced at only five meetings and, it seems, not at all in 1957. He did five in Formula 2 in 1958 – and retired.

By now he was firm friends with Alan Brown. 'He was a fabulous chap, very direct and very honest, the sort who you knew precisely where you stood with: left or right, right or wrong,' Brown says. 'He used to argue a lot – we had lots of arguments but they were always forgotten immediately afterwards. Basically he had a lot of common sense and he was a very easy partner. We got on very well.

'We decided to enter cars. I think he realised he wasn't going to be a great driver. He was quite good but when you are talking about fractions of seconds over a whole circuit you've got to be better than good. We joined forces with a friend who ran an engineering business and he put an equal amount of money in. We started entering cars. We looked at it as a business, in that it paid its way. We had a lot of fun and we had the opportunity to travel. After a time you stay with it or you get out. I decided that I'd had enough, but for him it was the beginning of team management.'

Tyrrell would say of his driving: 'I was always disappointed, cross with myself. And I couldn't go any quicker. The day when I began to manage a team, I knew that I had found my true path.'

How Tyrrell came to make the decision is clear. He accepted his driving limitations and it seems that this

Tyrrell was a genuine sports enthusiast who followed both the England cricket team and Spurs avidly. Evidently he also tried to play golf (Phipps/Sutton). Ken Tyrrell believed Grand Prix racing was about courage as well as skill. Here he talks to Bruce McLaren, bleeding from flying stones at the 1959 French Grand Prix, Reims.

centred around a specific moment during a Brands Hatch race. At least three versions survive.

One is recounted in *François Cevert, la mort dans mon contrat*: 'Ken was taking part in a race at Brands Hatch and, holding the steering wheel, had the impression of going so fast that he was admiring himself. Suddenly, in a corner where he thought he was on the limit, Ken saw another car stream past. Ken stopped at his pit; he waited for the end of the race. As soon as the chequered flag was lowered, he went to the driver who had overtaken him and said: "It's finished. You will never have problems in your life. From this moment on you will drive for me. Here is my car, I am your manager!" The young driver was called Bruce McLaren.'

One is recounted in a book about Bruce McLaren[5] where the author, Eoin Young, quotes Tyrrell as saying: 'Bruce had gone very well in practice and everyone was wondering who this new boy was. He really looked like a youngster then. I got a better start than he did and got out in front with him close behind. I remember thinking that he was going to have difficulty getting by, but then I imagined the commentator saying: "Why doesn't this old so-and-so Tyrrell get out of the way and let this youngster get on with

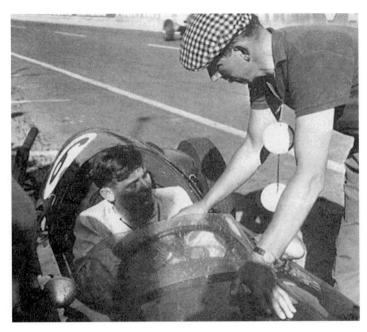

it?" so I moved over and let him by.'

The other is the race report of *Autosport* which wrote of Tyrrell, 'in Alan Brown's Cooper, taking an immediate lead with McLaren in second place. McLaren, anxious to show why he'd come to Britain's sunny clime, was steadily gaining on Tyrrell and on lap 6 passed him on Druids to pull out a convincing lead, which he held to the end.'

Tyrrell drove twice more, at Crystal Palace two weeks later and at Brands Hatch again, on 4 August when he finished seventh on aggregate.

It is true that a year later Tyrrell did sign McLaren to drive in Formula 2 for him. Neil Davis and a man called Alan Stait joined when Tyrrell 'set up the team', Davis says. 'I worked for him and Alan Brown and another guy on Formula 2 Coopers in 1959.'

Innocent days. The racing cars were prepared in a wooden hut at the timber yard which, evidently, was bought for £50 from the Women's Royal Army Corps. The hut was so rudimentary in appearance that Tyrrell was reluctant to show it to visitors, but inside it was surprisingly spacious with a working bench along one wall and the cars arranged beside the wall opposite. Reportedly, Walter Hayes – a very

important Ford executive – said: 'What a dump!' when he first saw it, but it was quiet and the mechanics could do their work without distractions.

Tyrrell believed that McLaren could become World Champion 'because he had the ability to think about it. He wasn't going to be the world's quickest driver, but then the world's quickest driver isn't always World Champion.'

The truth of this (initially) startling statement is revealed by a glance at those who have won the championship by determination and tactics rather than sheer speed alone: Graham Hill wasn't as quick as Jim Clark in 1962, Jody Scheckter wasn't as quick as Gilles Villeneuve in 1979, Keke Rosberg wasn't the quickest of a strong field in 1982, Alain Prost wasn't as quick as Ayrton Senna in 1989, and so it goes.

'To manage a team,' Tyrrell said many years later,[6] 'is within the capacity of any secretary who is a little bit gifted. I am not an engineer and I feel I am totally incapable of conceiving a racing car. I am not a businessman – which I regret. You don't believe me? I am going to tell you a story. François Guiter of Elf[7] said last New Year's Eve: "We'd already been financing you for three years when you decided to speak to me!" That said, it's true, I have never had the least problem with my sponsors ... but I have an explanation for that. It's because we win races!'

NOTES:
[1] Quote from *Ken Tyrrell, Surviving Formula 1*, A Mark Stewart Production, available from Duke.
[2] British Racing Motors, based in Bourne, Lincolnshire and 'founded as a trust intended to organize a co-operative industrial Grand Prix venture' (*Autocourse History of the Grand Prix Car, 1966-91*, Doug Nye, Hazleton Publishing 1992.)
[3] *Ken Tyrrell, Surviving Formula 1.*
[4] *Autosport*, 1 May 1953.
[5] *Bruce McLaren, The Man and His Racing Team* (Eoin S. Young, PSL, 1995).
[6] Quote from *François Cevert: la mort dans mon contrat* (Jean-Clauda Hallé, Editions J'ai Lu, Flammarion, 1974).
[7] François Guiter, marketing manager for Elf France and an important figure in French motorsport.

Chapter Two

JYS

'In 1964, Ken was no different than he was at the end of 1973 when I retired: the same man. He might have even had the same jacket and the same cap. The hands would be wrung the same way and he'd take no nonsense, had no memory – only todays and tomorrows.'

Sir Jackie Stewart

'Bob Mac came down with a young Scots fellow who pranced around, walked around on the balls of his feet making a general nuisance of himself. I didn't find out until a couple of years later that that young man was Jackie Stewart.'

Ken Tyrrell

'He put it into gear but unfortunately he didn't realise there was a Belgian copper – one of those with a tall hat on – standing on the footpath and whose eyes were sticking out like organ stops.'

Neil Davis

'In those early days it was fairly primitive down at the wood yard,' Neil Davis says. 'We had a workshop which he put up just for racing. It was cramped. We had three Formula 3 cars with BMC engines and there was just Alan Stait and myself. And that's how it was: very little equipment. Travelling? The mechanics drove the trucks. Well, we had a transporter – not quite a horsebox! The first one we bought was a three to five ton van, then we bought one of the ex-BRM Austins.

'And then we came across this shipload of buses that went down in the Thames Estuary on the way to Cuba. The ship sank and half the buses were under water but they salvaged it and brought all the buses back. They'd all rattled around against each other and the bodies were useless but

Stewart and Tyrrell in Germany – this time it's Ken's turn to listen (Schlegelmilch).

mechanically they were brand new, although admittedly, some of them had been in salt water.

'We went to an auction down in Essex somewhere. We didn't buy one at the auction because Ken felt there was a bit of a cartel going on. When he got back he rang the guy up who'd bought them all and he got one for the same price as this guy had paid for it. That was fitted with a body – a magnificent vehicle really, the pride and joy of the paddock, if you like. It was the first real custom-made transporter and on a coach chassis, so it was a lovely vehicle to drive.

'We had a hydraulic ramp on the back which lifted the cars. We could get two on the top and two on the bottom. You had a crew cab: behind the driver and passenger were two bunks which folded down into a seat, so if we were stuck out anywhere we could get our heads down. Ken was still working in the timber business and in fact he didn't pack that up until 1969. It started to get serious when Jackie came on board . . .'

The road to this, which began with Tyrrell's decision that he was never going to be good enough as a driver, is curious and, like so many tales drawn from the comparatively small motor racing community, tends to overlap and interlock.

In 1960, Tyrrell was running Formula Junior cars and knew that John Surtees[1], one of the most successful bike riders, was 'obviously thinking about turning to cars' – and by definition Grand Prix racing – 'and I read somewhere he had been driving the Aston Martin Formula 1 car, which was never any good.' (Surtees had tested two Astons, a sportscar and their F1 car, at the Goodwood circuit, Sussex, in late 1959 and early 1960. Surtees took his MV Agusta team-mate John Hartle[2] with him and Hartle drove it, too.)

Tyrrell rang Surtees, inviting him to 'come and drive for me'. Tyrrell reasoned that Surtees 'had to do some motor racing in order to be able to do Formula 1. You can't just go straight in. As a result of that, he came down to Goodwood

Opposite: The way it was. Brands Hatch (top) looking rural in 1962 at the start of a Formula 3 Junior race (Sutton). John Surtees (below left), here talking to Lotus boss Colin Chapman at Goodwood in 1961, began his car racing career with Tyrrell (Sutton). Jacky Ickx (below right) closes his eyes and contemplates victory. Tyrrell recognised his talent early and helped it blossom (Sutton).

and got into my Formula Junior car. He was a natural, absolutely, and that was clearly evident immediately. He was able to throw the car around, something that motorcyclists don't do. In fact a little later, I think at John's suggestion, I gave Bob McIntyre[3] a test down there. Bob came down with a young Scots fellow who pranced around, walked around on the balls of his feet making a general nuisance of himself. I didn't find out until a couple of years later that that young man was Jackie Stewart. He'd come down because he was a mate of Bob's.'

Stewart says: 'Bob Mac was a very good friend and he didn't know anything about motor car racing. He knew I knew something about it because of my brother, who'd driven before me[4]. He needed somebody to hold his hand, if you like, and be with him. It was a secret test that nobody knew about. I was the ideal person because (a) I wasn't a threat in the way his motorcycle colleagues might have been and (b), I was younger than Bobbie. I didn't know Ken Tyrrell at all. I mean, I knew who he was. I don't even know if he remembered me being there. My name wouldn't have meant anything to him.'

McIntyre explained the background in his autobiography[5]. 'One development I see is a closer link with the four-wheel game. John Surtees's switch from motorcycle racing to motor racing caused car racing teams to take a closer look at the two-wheel racers. Invitations to motor cyclists to try out cars followed. Mike Hailwood, John Hartle and Bob Anderson are all interested. I am too.'[6]

Stewart says: 'For me to be there with Bob was an awe-inspiring experience – to be at Goodwood at a private test for somebody who had never driven a four-wheel racing car before. He was a wonderful bike rider, and I knew all about his bike riding career.'

I recounted to Stewart what Tyrrell had said about him making a nuisance of himself and even – my memory must have betrayed me – of Tyrrell claiming Stewart did cartwheels. 'I think Ken's recall of that might have been slightly clouded. Cartwheels I never did!! I might have walked down to the chicane and watched him in the chicane – Ken and his team always used the first pit at Goodwood.'

'So,' Tyrrell said, 'Bob drove the car and he was useless,

A forgotten chapter of motor racing history: Tyrrell ran Minis! In 1962 (right) he had one in the Brands Hatch Six Hours for John Whitmore and Bill Blydenstein. Making a point to Whitmore (far right) before a 1962 race at Snetterton (MG Car Club). He also (left) ran two 'works-supported' Minis (his words) in the 1964 European Saloon Car Championship and the British Championship in 1965 (Phipps/Sutton).

absolutely bloody useless. Jackie said quite rightly to me afterwards – he wasn't Jackie Stewart to me then, just this little Scots fellow: "Bob's problem is that he's never had a car which can be driven properly. The only vehicle he ever drives is his Bedford van with his motorbikes in." Bob didn't know what it was to have an excess of power which made the back end come out, that sort of thing. And if a bike starts to move around you fall off it.'

Bob McIntyre 'crashed a five-speed experimental Norton at Oulton Park in August [1962] and died later from his injuries.'[7]

Surtees, recalling his test, told me that 'Ken is a person who gets wound up and goes off at all sorts of tangents, but basically he has a logical make-up, he can put two and two together. I think he thought there was nothing to lose, here's another rider who's very high in racing, might as well give him a go.'

Tyrrell, recalling their arrangement, said that 'what John undertook was to drive whenever he could. His father stood behind him all the time and what a pain in the backside his father was. "Don't sign anything, don't sign anything", he kept saying, but I didn't really need John to sign anything anyway! He first raced at Goodwood on Easter Monday and he came second to Jim Clark.'

Surtees would remember[8] that Tyrrell 'very kindly loaned me a Formula Junior Cooper-Austin for that meeting, and I agreed that I would drive it whenever my prior MV Augusta commitments permitted. Ken just happened to be there when when I made a visit to Cooper and, much later, he told me that it hadn't been a coincidence at all. John [Cooper] had telephoned him and told him to be there. It was also Ken who contacted the RAC to confirm what was needed for me to qualify for a licence.'

The race was Clark's first for Lotus, and he and Surtees had a determined duel for the lead, taking and re-taking each other. Clark set a new Formula Junior lap record but Surtees, who'd briefly been third, finished second.

'John has always been a bit of a difficult bloke, you know, but he never caused me any trouble,' Tyrrell said. 'The one race where he could have done really well – the British Empire Trophy at Silverstone – I think he must have had a commitment with his bike career which clashed. My

other driver was Henry Taylor[9], and Henry won Monaco, the traditional supporting race to the Grand Prix – which was then Formula Junior and almost the same as the Formula 3 it later became. Henry also won the British Empire Trophy. By then the Cooper with the BMC engine wasn't very competitive and we'd bought ourselves a Lotus with a Cosworth engine. Henry led from start to finish, which John could have done.'

Neil Davis was 'an apprentice at Coombs in Guildford [a garage which also ran racing cars] and Alan Brown was the sales manager there. He knew I was interested in motor racing and in 1958 I used to go up to his workshops in the evening and help the guy who was up there. I did one or two race meetings and Ken drove, I remember, at Crystal Palace. Then in 1959 I went full-time for Coombs and we had Masten Gregory and Bruce Mclaren driving two Coopers, which was really the works Formula 2 team, if you like. In 1960 Ken wanted to run his own outfit and set up his team. It was full-time. There were so many races all over the place. We raced Formula Junior from 1960 to 1964 or 1965 and the first year we had Surtees, Mike McGhee,

Henry Taylor and Keith Ballisat, who was the Shell competitions manager. The following year we had John Love and Tony Maggs and they raced for us for two years, then Timmy Mayer came on board but unfortunately Timmy – was to drive for us in 1964 – got killed in Australia in the Tasman series[10]. That's when Ken was looking around and found Jackie.'

In 1961, Maggs (a South African) and Love (a Rhodesian) largely dominated Formula Junior. Tyrrell, ruminating, would say it seemed funny because Love was thought to be old (in fact, born 1937) and yet four years after Tyrrell hired him he almost won the South African Grand Prix. Maggs, Tyrrell felt, had a 'classic approach – a beautiful style' while that of Love was more down-to-earth.

Maggs was second at Snetterton, won Goodwood, was third at Silverstone while Love won Chimay from Maggs; Maggs won Rouen from Love; Maggs won Karlskoga from Love, and the Roskilde Ring. Maggs won Zandvoort (Love unplaced) and Oulton (Love third). Then they did their double act at Montlhéry in the last race. One account of this 1961 season[11] says: 'The Tyrrell Racing Organisation spent most of the season across the Channel, with Tony Maggs and John Love as regular team drivers, But though their run of overseas victories was rarely checked (frequently they would take the first two places in a race), their occasional appearances at home did not meet with the same success. This indicated that the top British cars and drivers were still the most formidable Formula Junior competitors.'

Maggs and Love stayed for 1962 and there's a lovely tale from Neil Davis about a race at Chimay, a circuit in Belgium near the French frontier. 'We were using Belgian fuel and after a few laps we were holing pistons because the fuel was detonating. Ken and Alan Stait and myself sat down and said: "What are we going to do?" It was suggested that we lower the compression ratio by putting two head gaskets on it etc, and then Ken said he was going to talk to the guy who did the engines at BMC[12]. He came back about an hour later.'

Tyrrell: 'Neil, I want you to come with me. We are going to Zandvoort.'

Davis: 'What are we going to Zandvoort for, Ken?'

Tyrrell: 'Because the Formula 1 race is up there and I've spoken to John Cooper. He is going to get a load of fuel from Shell and we'll pick up that fuel – it will be 100 octane and we won't have a problem.'

Tyrrell had a Zephyr and off he and Davis went. 'From the French border it's got to be 200 miles to Zandvoort. We get there, meet John Cooper, and fill the boot up with two-gallon petrol cans and put some on the back seat as well. Off we go, back. I've been driving then Ken took over and in the early hours of the morning – it was just getting daylight – the roads were pretty damp. Ken was driving and we rushed into this Belgian village and we came off the tarmac on to cobbles. There was an S-bend in the middle of this village. We scrabbled round the first of it but lost it right the way round the second part. God must have been on our side: we didn't hit anything.

'He put it into gear but unfortunately he didn't realise there was a Belgian copper – one of those with a tall hat on – standing on the footpath and whose eyes were sticking out like organ stops. As we drove away he got his whistle out and blew like hell. Ken said: "Well, we're not going to stop" so off down the road we go. I said: "We'd better do something about this, Ken. We've got to get off the road – they'll have a roadblock." We got the map out, detoured for about ten miles and got back on. We arrived at Chimay fairly early on the morning, put the petrol in and finished first and second. That was how organised and determined Ken was – drive all the way overnight. A lot of people would have said: "Nothing we can do," but not Ken. He was like a Jack Russell with a rat when he got hold of something. He would never let go until it was sorted.'

And yes, it got serious when Jackie came . . .

'In 1963, I was racing for Ecurie Ecosse in a Cooper Monaco,' Stewart says. The episode which changed everything happened at Goodwood although Stewart can't remember whether it happened in testing or in a race. He drove the Cooper Monaco in four races – Snetterton, Oulton, Goodwood in September, and Charterhall, winning them all.

At Goodwood, 'I had given John Coundley in a Lotus 19, which was the state-of-the-art sports car, a hard time and had been leading him. Robin McKay was the track manager and he called Ken, because Ken was always a big talent spotter. He had a long, long history of that. In 1963, I had won more British national races than any other driver in a variety of different cars. Ken had heard only about the one drive I had made, at Goodwood, from Robin.'

'I had a phone call from Robin McKay,' Tyrrell would say. 'He called about this young Scotsman driving an out-of-date sports car round Goodwood and driving it with some verve.' The implication: give him a test.

Graham Gauld[13] would write that 'early in January 1964 David Murray[14] discussed with Jackie Stewart the plans for the season and forwarded to him a written contract which Jackie signed on March 4. Shortly after this, however, I received a telephone call from Jackie to say he had been telephoned by Ken Tyrrell to ask whether he would go south and test a Formula 3 Cooper with a view to driving for Tyrrell in 1964, and what did I think! Obviously I was

Tyrrell's first big win as a team manager: Monaco, 1960, and the Formula Junior race. The Lotuses of (from left) Peter Arundell, Jim Clark and Trevor Taylor fill the front row – but Henry Taylor (no 150) beat them all . . . Here is Henry Taylor with Tyrrell after the race (Martin Hadwen, Motor Racing Archive).

flattered and with no hesitation I said he would be daft if he didn't at least go down for the test. He answered by saying that he had put the same question to his brother Jimmy and to David Murray and they had said the same thing.'

Far away in Tasmania, Mayer had been killed on 28 February. Tyrrell conceded that, in 1963, Mayer had not enjoyed the success he deserved because the team had a poor engine but described him as a 'marvellous driver' and a potential world champion.

Anyway, John Young Stewart, known as Jackie, travelled down to Goodwood for Tyrrell's Formula 3 car and the test.

Tyrrell had Bruce McLaren there to set a time, a familiar arrangement on occasions like this. The experienced driver takes the car out and lays down a benchmark against which the youngster, in the same car, can be judged. Stewart remembers meeting Tyrrell and seeing 'how professional he was, how authoritative.'

Tyrrell 'lectured' him about not rushing it: 'take you time, we're all day'. 'Jackie went off and did a few laps,' Tyrrell would say, 'and after half a dozen laps he was going quicker than Bruce, whereupon Bruce said: "Let me get back in that motorcar." He went faster. Stewart went back out – and faster again. Bruce said: "This is ridiculous. Let me get back in that car" – and then he went quicker again. This went on all day and Stewart ended up with the quickest time. John

Cooper was there. He took me to one side and said "that boy's good. Get him signed up quick." So we did.'

Neil Davis confirms it. 'John was walking round the circuit, and although I didn't hear the conversation I understand he came back and said to Ken: "You'd better sign him up quick."' Jackie Stewart confirms it, too. 'Bruce McLaren was at that time the Formula 1 factory driver for Cooper and I had no idea what I was doing. Going quicker than Bruce McLaren, that was unthinkable for me. It wasn't as if I thought I was good: I was confused, very confused. John Cooper was there himself and he said "you've got to sign him now."'

Stewart went back to Tyrrell's house, sat there and they talked. 'I had gone quite well. He made me the offer but I didn't accept that day, I accepted the next day. He offered me two contracts: one for £5 [and Stewart kept all winnings] or one for £10,000 but for which he would take 10 per cent of my future income for ten years.

'I had no money. At that time Helen and I would not have had fifty quid between us in the bank, and £10,000 in March of 1964 was an incredible amount of money. He said: "You've got these two options but either way I still want you to drive for me." The £5 option, incidentally, was the tender for a contract to be legal. I said: "Well, I'd like to think about it."

'I went away that night and did think about it. I called him next morning and I said "I will sign for you but I'll just take the £5." I reasoned that if he was offering me 10% of £10,000 there must be more money in this business than I was aware of. Ken was being clever, and he never said: "You either take the deal I'm offering or I won't have you drive for me." Within ten days I was in the first Formula 3 race I did for him, at Snetterton in absolutely torrential rain. It was the day that Graham Hill crashed at Coram Curve.'[15]

In fact, there was a Formula 1 race with a strong entry (Clark, Hill, Peter Arundell, Bruce McLaren, Jack Brabham, Jo Bonnier, Phil Hill). Graham Hill lost a wheel and the resultant crash was so spectacular that Hill was fortunate to escape uninjured. Stewart remembers Hill's BRM 'up in the air and crashing heavily'. Innes Ireland went on to win the race from Jo Bonnier.

A driver called John Fenning was fastest in practice for the Formula 3 race, Stewart next. Stewart took 'an immediate lead' in the race 'and was the only one to avoid heavy baulking' at Riches and Coram on the first lap. Stewart, alone, built up a good lead, never lost it and set fastest lap. The race finished: Stewart 21m 20.0s (76.22mph), Fenning (Lotus-BMC) (no time) but 44 seconds behind.

The Stewart era had begun.

'I earned £186 in that one race – I didn't have that kind of money!' Stewart says. 'In that year we won the British Formula 3 Championship, we won the European Formula 3 Championship and we won the Monaco Formula 3 race which was very important. That year I drove in 53 races in 26 different racing cars – and won 23 – but that included Formula 1. That year I drove all these racing cars and I think I am right in saying I made £10,500. I drove everything!' (Neil Davis adds to this. 'The mechanics got 10 per cent of the driver's winnings and that went on for quite a number of years. In fact, it was only when we went into Formula 1 that we didn't get that.')

Bill Gavin, covering the Monaco race for *Autosport*, wrote that Stewart 'scored a most convincing win in the first major international event to be run in the new Formula 3. The Swiss Silvio Moser . . . was the only driver to challenge Stewart at any time.'

The drivers were divided into two heats, both run before the Formula 1 final practice on the Saturday afternoon. Stewart won the first heat and Moser the second, so they lined up on the front row for the 'final', which began at 6 o'clock that evening. However, Stewart had covered the 16 laps of his heat some eight seconds faster than Moser had done his. Moser beat Stewart to Ste Devote, but by the third lap Stewart had overtaken him. Gavin noted how relaxed

Stewart's style seemed and 'the stop watch was the only indication that he was going so much faster than the rest of the field.'

The great ones often seem to have time to go fast slowly. Stewart 42m 35.0s . . . Moser 42m 52s.

Ken Tyrrell had found a gem. So had Stewart.

'In 1964, Ken was no different than he was at the end of 1973 when I retired: the same man,' Stewart says. 'He might have even had the same jacket and same cap. The hands would be wrung the same way and he'd take no nonsense, had no memory – only todays and tomorrows. When he gave you a real froth job he had lost his temper. He was aggressive with his voice and that was him losing his temper – but it was a short one, and then it just blew away.'

Neil Davis echoes that. 'Ken was the same when he employed me as when he retired. Straight down the middle, down-to-earth, honest as the day is long. What he said was gospel and that was it. Good guy. A very, very trustworthy, honest person. He did give people bollockings. He'd say "and what are you going to do about it?" I'd say: "Well, we'll do whatever you want, Ken, I suppose. You're the boss." And then off he'd go. About an hour later he'd come back and say: "Fancy a bit of lunch up the pub, Neil?" and it was gone, gone, finished. He'd said what he had to say, end of story.'

'It was quite a small operation in those days,' Stewart reflects, 'but he was the best team manager that I ever was exposed to and I had some pretty good people. He told you exactly how things were, you told him the same – we were totally, honest, frank and in total confidence of each other. I trusted him implicitly. We had quite a few disagreements – I got the famous froth job. When you got it, you got it and then ten seconds later it had gone, so therefore he was never a man who harboured a grudge: nothing was protracted. [After the initial year and the £5] we didn't have a contract and I would never have needed a contract with Ken Tyrrell. The first one was the only written one.' Stewart's partner this season, incidentally was one Warwick Banks[16] and, evidently, all Tyrrell's diplomacy was needed to mollify Banks that he was getting the same equipment as Stewart.

Tyrrell would say that Stewart won Monaco 'so easily that it was thoroughly outstanding.' That season Stewart won the Formula Junior Championship (well, one of them: there were two with different sponsors) and Stewart says: 'My fondest memory? So many. The Formula 3 days because it was so fresh and so new, and he was like a father to me. I was so lacking in knowledge and experience, which meant I relied on him even more.'

'We then moved on to Formula 2 [in 1965] which was a bit more glamorous than Formula 3 and we were racing against Jochen Rindt, Graham Hill, and of course Jimmy Clark,' Tyrrell would say.

Although Stewart drove elsewhere from 1965 to 1968, when Tyrrell entered Grand Prix racing, he continued to drive for Tyrrell, too, in Formula 2. As Stewart says, 'Tyrrell started the Cooper factory Formula 2 car with a BRM engine, so there was an alliance there and he ran that operation. [Cooper had been hurt in a road crash.] Eventually he made it to the Matra with the Ford engine. So I stayed with Ken from 1964 – I was driving the Formula 2 while I was driving the Formula 1 BRM.'

In 1965, Tyrrell was running the Cooper cars but 'with little success. Their spaceframe chassis were by that time uncompetitive.' At the end of that year Tyrrell went to Paris for the French Formula 2 prize-giving ceremony at BP's headquarters, and it opened the way to Matra.

Neil Davis says that 'after I'd been to Matra, the difference with Cooper was complete – the engineering, the people, the way everything was constructed. Matra was vast. It was another world. We'd seen the BRM and Cooper Formula 1 cars, but Matra was a Rolls-Royce against a Ford. Ken rang me up one day after meeting a guy called Lagardère[17]. He was introduced by Jabby Crombac[18] and Ken called me the next day. "I want you to go to Paris and I want you to take an engine and gearbox with you." I said: "What?" He said: "I want you to go to Matra. You will be met just outside Paris and they will steer you in."' Davis went and 'we fitted this Formula 2 engine – a Cosworth – into a Matra car which they in turn flew in a Bristol Freighter to Goodwood. And Jackie tried it. His first impression was that he had never driven a car like

A partnership to conquer the world: Tyrrell and a very young-looking Jackie Stewart (Sutton). . . . The prettiest pit lane crew of all: Norah Tyrrell (left) keeping an eye on lap times, with Helen Stewart, here at the 1968 Dutch Grand Prix (Sutton).

it: you put the power down and it did everything right.

'It just went from there. The following year we were running Formula 2 Matras and we had a Formula 3 for Jacky Ickx. The year after that – 1967 – we had the 1600 FVA [Ford] engine, a very good engine, and Matra made a very good car to go with it. That was the year Ickx was the European Formula 2 Champion and Jackie won four or five races.'

Tyrrell felt that saloon car drivers had difficulty adapting to single-seaters but he'd seen Ickx, a young Belgian, racing a Lotus Cortina and signed him because 'he was so composed in time of drama'. Some unrecorded incident had damaged the Cortina so badly that a front wheel was hanging off. Ickx arrived in the pits perfectly composed – Tyrrell had anticipated Ickx would have been gesticulating and howling. And Ickx was quick, quick enough to warrant a test – which he passed – and be given a drive in 1966 (he was doing his National Service in 1965).

This is what Ickx says. 'Ah, Ken. I was just thinking about him the other day. He was not only part of my life but also part of my destiny. Without him, no doubt I would not have reached the goals I did reach in motorsport. He found me in an unbelievable place – in 1964 in Budapest when I was driving the Lotus Cortina. Apparently he liked my style or my behaviour or whatever. He felt I was good. He offered me a test of one of his Cooper Formula 3 or Formula 2 cars at Goodwood and I had to decline it because I was going in to the army to do my National Service. Unfortunately I had to say: "I am sorry, I cannot do anything for a year." He said: "Don't worry, I'll call you back in a year's time" – and he did.

'Then we went to Goodwood because at the time Goodwood was a place where everyone tried their cars. I went once or twice there in October 1965 and I made a huge number of spins. Finally I destroyed that Cooper in the fence on one of the fastest corners. He still believed I was not that bad and then we tried again at Oulton Park with the first Matra Formula 3. That I destroyed, too. I was fighting with Beltoise who had the same car. He was going three times faster than me, I was three times faster than him

afterwards and finally – again – I crashed the car. Although I was searching for the limits and it was very costly for him, he didn't change his opinion of me, so I went with him in 1966 and 1967.

'He treated me, I think, as a son. He already understood, before a lot of other people did, the psychology of the relationship between a team boss and a driver: it is important to be loved to be fast. He forgave me all my mistakes! That is why I say he was the man who had the key to my starting – and the confidence, too.

'In 1967, I was European Formula 2 Champion. At the time I did very little Formula 3 but a lot of Formula 2. When Jackie Stewart was driving Formula 1 I could drive his car – it was better than mine – and we mixed old and new chassis. The Championship was a good one then and I beat a number of people who were good[19]. I must say that the Matra, Ken Tyrrell and the Dunlop tyres made the difference. We had a lot of fun at, for example, Zandvoort because this Formula 2 car was faster than the Formula 1 cars had been the year before!'

Jack Brabham had taken pole with a lap of 1m 28.1s in 1966, now Ickx took pole with 1m 27.5s in Formula 2[20].

That race was some seven weeks after the Dutch Grand Prix. Tyrrell had flown to it because Ford's new Formula 1 Cosworth engine was making its début. When he flew back he had made two decisions. The first was that he must have a Cosworth, the second that he must have a Formula 1 car to put it in. He didn't have a driver, but never mind.

The Tyrrell Grand Prix team was about to be born.

NOTES:

[1] *Champions* by Hilton and John Blunsden (MRP, 1993)

[2] MV – Meccanica Verghera – was an Italian company founded in 1945 and between 1952 and 1977 their bikes won 37 world titles. John Hartle, a Briton, from Chapel-en-le-Frith, was a leading rider between 1955 and the 1960s. He won three 500cc World Championship races.

[3] Bob McIntyre, a Glaswegian, was a gifted rider who was the first man to average 100mph in a TT race on the Isle of Man in 1957, the year he just missed the 500cc World Championship.

4 Jimmy Stewart, the elder Stewart brother (born 1931, Jackie 1939), had a solid career as a sports car driver (and one Grand Prix, Britain, 1953) before he crashed in 1955 and retired.

5 *Motor Cycling Today* by Bob McIntyre (Arthur Barker, 1962).

6 Mike Hailwood was arguably the greatest bike racer of all, famed for charisma, versatility, good living – and winning nine world titles.

7 *Great Motor-Cycle Riders* by Peter Carrick (Hale, 1985).

8 *John Surtees, World Champion* by John Surtees and Alan Henry (Hazleton Publishing, 1991).

9 Henry Taylor, a Briton and a farmer, began racing in 1954 and took part in eight Grands Prix between 1959 and 1961.

10 Tim Mayer was an American and a graduate of Yale whose career began in 1959 in an Austin-Healey. He drove a single Grand Prix, the US, in 1962. He was killed when he crashed in the Tasman series in Tasmania.

11 *Motor Racing Year 1961* by Blunsden and Alan Brinton (Knightsbridge, 1961).

12 British Motor Corporation (BMC), once a major manufacturer.

13 *Ecurie Ecosse, A Social History of Motor Racing from the Fifties to the Nineties* by Graham Gauld (Graham Gauld Public Relations, 1992).

14 David Murray, an Edinburgh accountant, drove in four Grands Prix between 1950 and 1952 and set up Ecurie Ecosse, a successful sports car team.

15 Coram, the big right-hander leading to the start-finish straight.

16 Warwick Banks, a British driver born in 1939.

17 Jean-Luc Lagardère, general manager of the Sports Division.

18 Crombac, one of the most senior and respected motor sport journalists, who worked for *Sport Auto* in Paris. He had been very close to Colin Chapman and Jim Clark.

19 The Championship finished Ickx 45 (41 counting), Frank Gardner 33, Beltoise 27, Piers Courage 24, Alan Rees 23, Chris Irwin and Johnny Servoz-Gavin 15.

20 Ickx also had some fun at the Nürburgring where Formula 2 cars were included in the Grand Prix. He qualified the Matra third! (Clark pole, 8m 04.1s, Denny Hulme's Brabham-Repco 8m 13.5s, Ickx 8m 14.0s). 'That car was really flying. It was a place I knew very well and that was the launch for me into Formula 1. I was very fast at the Nürburgring. I was almost 30 seconds faster than the next Formula 2 car, which was Jackie Oliver. You have to understand that Formula 1 cars at the Nürburgring were very difficult to drive although they had more power and so on. It was also a matter of timing and compromise and the perfect solution was that Formula 2 car. If Stewart or Clark had driven it, maybe it would have been on pole!'

Chapter Three

WORLD BEATERS

"Ken said "come and drive for me" and I said "you don't have a car, Ken!""

Sir Jackie Stewart

'*After the race a local company would give the weight of the driver in chocolates to charity. They had this weigh bridge set up. We filled Stewart's pockets with spanners and all sorts of things. He walked to the scales like a deep sea diver, sat on them and they could not believe how heavy he was.*'

Neil Davis

'*You are going to take part in your first Grand Prix. It is necessary for you to know that you have nothing to prove. Anyway, you have no chance of winning. I absolutely want that you drive within yourself, without taking any risks.*'

Ken Tyrrell

'I was going to go to Ferrari and I pulled out,' Stewart says. 'Enzo Ferrari offered me a deal and then moved the deal round because he thought I was asking for too much money. I didn't have anywhere to go. Ken said: "Come and drive for me" and I said: "You don't have a car, Ken!" He had a Cosworth DFV because that had become available – he went to Zandvoort and ordered the engine without having anything to put it in.'

Or, as Neil Davis puts it, 'Ken was always very approachable, a very friendly man and Norah was like that, too. It was a family, you were part of the family and that's how it was run. I wanted to go Formula 1, without a doubt. At the end of 1967, Ken said: "I'm thinking of going Formula 1 and I've ordered the engines from Cosworth

Stewart in Holland, 1971, where he finished eleventh – and cut some corners very fine! (Schlegelmilch).

37

already." And he didn't even have a driver at that time – I don't think Jackie had agreed!'

Stewart emphasises the temptation of the Cosworth engine, and its value to the whole of Grand Prix racing. 'There was no differentiation between all the Ford engines. You went up there, you paid £7,500 and you got an engine. It wasn't, say, like having a turbo when the others didn't, it was definitely more level ground between the competitors and there was no doubting that. The Ford Cosworth engine was so regular, although you had to drive very well and you had to have a very good chassis.'

Jacky Ickx might have gone into Formula 1 with Tyrrell but joined Ferrari instead. 'I think he had a lot of wishes for it,' Ickx says, 'and I had the same wishes for it.

Story of a season . . . 1968, and Tyrrell's first in Grand Prix racing. Johnny Servoz-Gavin in the Matra at Monaco, a race he ought to have won (Phipps/ Sutton).

Unfortunately there were only two chassis available for Formula 1 – for Jackie and the other for a Frenchman – Beltoise. It had to be a Frenchman. We were very sad and we never really talked about it later on. I must say that I really feel extremely grateful, unbelievably grateful, because I think it's true to say that without him no-way could I have done what I have done. Ken never liked the high life in my opinion, he was very efficient and very human at the same time. He was not interested in the past, only in the present and the future. Yesterday was yesterday and there's nothing you can do about it . . .'

The first Grand Prix of 1968 was the South African at Kyalami on 1 January, which meant that there was virtually no time for Matra to refine their Formula 1 car for the Cosworth DFV engine – in fact Matra had only competed in three Grands Prix, Monaco, the USA and Mexico in 1967.

'We collected our first DFV and took it over to Matra,' Neil Davis says. 'We fitted it in with no intention of going to the first race in Formula 1 because there were various problems. We didn't have a starter on it and so on. We intended to take a Formula 2 car with a big weight along the bottom to make the regulations. We went off to Montlhéry[1] with the Formula 1 and did a test there and after the test Jackie said: "We've really got to take this" so we went back to Matra. They scratched their heads and

found a way: we put a universal joint in so we could put the starter at an angle, and we got it up to a standard that covered all the regs. We took it to Kyalami for the first race more or less straight out of the box and it qualified third. He was running in third place and the engine went [a connecting rod broke on lap 44] but we had proved we were competitive – and we knew we were. We should have won the championship that year and if Jackie hadn't broken a bone in his wrist I am sure we would have.'

Stewart crashed at Jarama during practice for a Formula 2 race, and missed the Spanish and Monte Carlo Grands Prix. Jean-Pierre Beltoise deputised in Spain. 'According to my memory,' Beltoise says, 'I was leading but unfortunately there was a problem with the car. I replaced Jackie Stewart who'd hurt himself and I got in because Tyrrell were using a Matra.' Beltoise was close to Matra – and he did lead, but had an engine problem and finished fifth.

Another Frenchman, Johnny Servoz-Gavin, deputised at Monaco. He had driven for Tyrrell in Formula 2 (and would, in 1969, become Formula 2 Champion 'in a Matra, but prepared in England'). 'I was very happy in Formula 2. Ken was an Englishman, didn't speak a word of French. Never. We managed, in the way that Frenchmen do manage in English. He was a gentleman, exactly. I believe that all the drivers who drove for him recognised that he was both a gentleman and a father figure at the same time.'

Tyrrell used Stewart to give Servoz-Gavin instructions, because Tyrrell knew he would listen to Stewart. 'I had to have Johnny after qualifying and after the morning of the race telling him what Ken wanted me to tell him. I would have told him anyway! Ken was quite forceful when he wanted to tell you something but he never told you how to drive. And the car was just perfect for Monaco, it would have won – Johnny led the first lap [but hit the chicane and the driveshaft failed]. Using me to tell Johnny, because Johnny would listen to me? That's a shrewd thing to do, isn't it?'

Servoz-Gavin confirms that Stewart gave him advice, especially since the car was Stewart's. Servoz-Gavin found Stewart wise and a good guy. Interestingly, Servoz-Gavin and Beltoise had competed in Monaco the year before in Formula 2 Matras but ballasted up to make the Formula 1

weight. Now, in Stewart's car, Servoz-Gavin lined up on the front row next to Graham Hill (Lotus, pole) and was faster to Ste Devote. He led. 'When you have a good car, it is always easy [chuckle]. Unfortunately, I touched the pavement [chuckle].' This seems to have damaged the car, the driveshaft breaking on lap 4.

Davis feels that 'the biggest disappointment was when we were leading Spa (the fourth race and Stewart's first after the crash). Before the race started Ken had done all the fuel calculations. In the position that we had the metering unit set, the car was very difficult – it didn't have a lot of driveability out of the pits, it had a hesitancy. So Ken said

we'd just rich it up a bit but, unbeknown, we made a mistake because every notch up was one per cent more fuel you needed. We were new at the game, weren't we?'

With four laps to go, Stewart led Bruce McLaren by 29.5 seconds. McLaren was in fact catching him but at nothing like the speed needed to overhaul him.

'With two laps to go, the Dunlop manager started bringing champagne into the back of the pits, stacking it up there,' Davis says. 'We ran out of fuel with one lap to go – we did manage to get some fuel into it, but . . . '

Stewart coasted into the pits and 'a couple of gallons were hastily added.'[2] By then McLaren, Pedro Rodriguez and Jacky Ickx had gone by and, worse, Stewart's battery was flat. Eventually he emerged and completed the lap but it was disallowed because it was more than double the time of the fastest lap. *Autosport* reported that 'apparently Ken Tyrrell had expected the Matra to consume fuel at 7mpg and it had averaged nearer 6.6mpg.'

Neil Davis remembers: 'We were in the back of the transporter after the race. There was Ken, there was Norah, Roger Hill, myself, Max Rutherford and Keith Boshier and we were all crying our eyes out.'

The first win, so important for so many reasons, had been within their grasp.

They only had to wait two weeks for it. Stewart put the Matra on the second row at Zandvoort and won the Dutch Grand Prix by an astonishing 1 minute 33.93 seconds from Beltoise (in the Matra factory car). Nobody else finished on the same lap. The race was run in atrocious weather and Stewart actually lapped everyone before Beltoise unlapped himself towards the end. To win by such a margin in such conditions is the mark of a master.

An aside here. I once had the temerity to suggest to Tyrrell that a certain track – I think the street circuit of Detroit – should be taken off the Grand Prix calendar because, frankly, it was farcical: it had manhole covers, no atmosphere and was so cramped that Formula 1 cars were quite unable to show what they could do there, much to the apathy of The Great American Public. 'Nonsense!' he said. I got the froth job. 'I will tell you that a Formula 1 driver and a Formula 1 car should be able to drive anywhere – Monaco or Monza, street circuits, fast circuits out in the country, the lot. It's no good them – or you – moaning the whole time – because doing that is what makes it a world championship. I will tell you something else. A Formula 1 driver should be able to master whatever conditions he is confronted with. That's what makes it a world championship, too! All right?'

Hilton (meekly): 'Yes.'

Stewart was to prove this in Germany.

If Holland had been bad, the Nürburgring was a brooding, shrouded monster lashed by rain. Of the three practice sessions, Friday morning was swallowed by fog and Friday afternoon abandoned because, in the murk, nobody could see very much at all. On the Saturday, the track didn't open to the cars until 3 o'clock and, in what passed for final practice, Stewart set fastest time.

The organisers decided on an extra practice session on the Sunday morning although essentially the track was flooded and who knew where, in this grey, standing water stood? Worse, the rain had dragged mud across the track and mud would act like ice.

Stewart was extremely reluctant to go out in this, and understandably so, not least because he had had a terrible crash at Spa in 1966 and was becoming the spokesman for safety. Tyrrell ordered him to go out, the only time he ever did such a thing. He'd explain to Stewart that unless he went out he wouldn't know where the standing water and the mud were. Stewart went fastest.

(There is an exquisite irony here. I wondered if Tyrrell ever gave Stewart advice before a race, in the sense that Stewart was a master driver and Tyrrell manifestly had not been. Unthinkingly, I used the Nürburgring as an example – not this race but in general. Stewart said Tyrrell might say something like: 'You know, take it easy.' Not on the morning of 4 August, 1968, though).

He lined up on the third row because, by a paradox, the Friday morning times – with the circuit under fog but not awash – were much faster than the other two sessions, and he hadn't done a good time. Icky, incidentally, had pole in the Ferrari. Stewart made a good start, gaining places immediately, and took the lead by Schwalbenschwanz, a right-left-left-right contortion 12 miles out. He led at the end of this first lap by eight seconds, increased it to 25 after lap 2 and 37 after lap 3. Thereafter he built and built on it and won by 4m 03.2s from Graham Hill (Lotus). Tyrrell, under an umbrella, stood waiting for a long, long time for Hill to come by.

'The weather was so bad that the springs wouldn't open when you pushed the throttle – they were jammed up,' Neil Davis says. 'Jackie explained: "For the last couple of laps I

Story of a season: Tyrrell's first win ought to have come in Belgium (top) but a fuel miscalculation thwarted Stewart. The team only had to wait two weeks to the Dutch Grand Prix. Stewart won by more than a minute and a half. Tyrrell here making sure he has enough fuel? (all Sutton).

*Story of a season
. . . One of the
greatest victories in
Formula 1 history.
Stewart rides the
elements at the
Nürburgring and
wins the 1968
German Grand
Prix by more than
four minutes
(all Sutton).*

have been driving on the ignition switch." Driving on the ignition switch round the Nürburgring – can you imagine that? And to win by four minutes – fantastic!

'After the race a local company were giving the weight of the winning driver in chocolates to charity. They had this weigh bridge set up. We filled up Stewart's pockets with spanners and all sorts of things. He walked to the scales like a deep sea diver, sat on them and they could not believe how heavy he was. I mean, he probably weighed eight and a half stone and we got him up to something like eleven!'

Stewart finished the season second in the Championship to Graham Hill. He'd been partnered by Servoz-Gavin for four of the races and in 1969 he'd be partnered by Beltoise with Servoz-Gavin doing the last three races as well. It scarcely mattered: Stewart dominated the season absolutely, winning South Africa, Spain, Holland, France, Britain and coming second in Germany. Stewart has captured the atmosphere within the team[3] so neatly that it is worth reproducing.

Story of a season . . . Jean-Pierre Beltoise moving towards fifth place in the 1968 Italian Grand Prix (top) and Tyrrell surveys Stewart's car in Canada, while Norah notes every detail from the pit wall.

'All the major work on the car was done at Matra's works at Velizy near Paris. When, for example, the car was shunted at Silverstone [in practice] it went back to the works to be rebuilt, but otherwise all race preparation was done by Ken's mechanics [at the timber yard factory]. During races, Ken managed the pit and timed me, and Bruno [Morin of Matra] timed Jean-Pierre. Norah kept the lap chart, which is the difficult bit. Ken's son, Kenneth, who flew as a second officer for BEA in Tridents, usually managed to get his duties to coincide with races in Europe, and he invariably brought as good a weather forecast with him as anyone can get.'

From this – the family atmosphere – came the Championship.

Beltoise tells it from a slightly different angle. 'I went to Tyrrell, I believe, because the Matra wasn't quite ready. It was an agreement between Matra and Tyrrell. I was very happy because Ken Tyrrell had plenty of experience and Matra had just begun in competition. Tyrrell were fairly new into Formula 1 but more 'run in' [in motoring terms!]

than Matra.

'With Ken, my relationship was always very, very good. We understood each other well and Norah would tell you that. I learnt English at school and I worked on it a bit. Ken was very rigorous, very professional – a great professional – and that's important. I like things which are straightforward, clear and with Ken Tyrrell it was always straightforward, always clear – with Jackie, too, because Jackie had a sense of friendship about him and certainly he was a winner and had more experience than me. Thus I was behind him – not far behind him, although he was a great champion. Jackie helped me all the time and when it was necessary he gave me judicious advice.

'This was notable at Spa. Jackie offered wise counsel – because Spa was dangerous. He said: "Jean-Pierre, at this place you don't do this and at that place you don't do that because it's too dangerous." He was a good bloke. At that time it was impossible for me to beat him. The thing that impressed me enormously was Stewart at the Nürburgring in 1968 when he was untouchable. It was a difficult circuit anyway, but above all in those conditions that year – the fog, the rain, almost a storm the whole weekend. I remember how difficult it was and I was enormously impressed by Jackie's performance.

'You have to remember that the car was good but because I lacked experience I was still discovering the circuits. It was my first true season in Formula 1 and I was very happy. The memory of it still makes me happy.'

Beltoise joined Matra for 1970 but his relationship with Tyrrell remained warm across the years to come. 'When my son Julian wanted to drive, I asked Ken to look after him at the start of the season. In his holidays he went to the races with Tyrrell. Ken was between a father and an uncle – he was exactly that. And then of course he was close to my brother-in-law François Cevert, and he became a friend of the whole family, almost a member of the family.'

In 1970, everything changed. Matra refused to build a car for the Cosworth engine and so Tyrrell got March to do it instead, as a holding operation until he could build his own cars. In that sense the 1970 season was one of

The partnership with Goodyear. . . Tyre testing at Interlagos (left), Tyrrell and Bert Baldwin deep in conversation at Kyalami, and the Goodyear team (all Bert Baldwin).

anticipation rather than fulfillment, Stewart finished the championship joint fifth.

Servoz-Gavin left, too. As Stewart puts it, 'in the end he was into having to have yoga before the races, sitting on the floor of the transporter with all the doors closed. He had wound himself up very tight. He was a special guy, very skilled and talented in natural ability but his mind management wasn't so good. He had a magnificent yacht – far too big! Lots of birds, yes.'

Servoz-Gavin did not qualify for Monaco and promptly retired. 'His decision came as a total surprise to me,' Tyrrell said[4], 'although the last few times Johnny wasn't really competitive any more – he drove badly at Monaco. He threw a great party to celebrate his non-qualification. That should have alerted me.'

These many years later, Servoz-Gavin explains that he'd driven for Tyrrell only 11 times between 1968 and 1970 because, as the team's third driver, they needed three race cars and a spare – and didn't always have them. 'I was only there when a third car was available. A sad situation? It wasn't too bad.' He adds: 'I had a problem with one eye and I couldn't 'work' well any more. I preferred to stop because it was dangerous. Yes, Ken was surprised when I had a party [chuckle] after I failed to qualify . . .'

Tyrrell needed a replacement and, two weeks after Monaco, he and Stewart went to Crystal Palace to watch the Formula 2 race there. François Guiter had already told him to keep an eye on a young Frenchman who was good. He was called François Cevert.

'I went there,' Tyrrell would say, 'to look at possible candidates. Cevert was high on my list but Jackie, who had raced against him, had already drawn my attention to him. I had followed his results in the press but I was not absolutely certain that this boy could become a real racing driver. He didn't have the right profile: too handsome, too joyous, too happy – but maybe I was wrong.' Norah said simply of Cevert: 'He is as handsome as a god.'

Cevert was so timid that he only said 'hello' to Tyrrell and later confessed: 'Tyrrell's reputation is such that, if you have something to do with him, you feel you are small.'

The man who wrote Cevert's biography, Jean-Claude Hallé, set down this lovely description of Tyrrell himself. 'Norah Tyrrell could have been born in any country north of the 45th parallel, but the minute her husband appears there is no doubt: this man is English – and even a caricature of an Englishman. He has kept the stature of his origins: the physique of a big lumberjack, with a red nose, with the large teeth of a horse, with hair which is difficult to keep under control – a tuft constantly falls over his eye. Precise, practical, in a hurry, courteous in his relations despite a difficult manner, Ken Tyrrell is a prodigious person.'

Stewart drove in Belgium while Cevert waited for his phone to ring. He stayed in his Parisian flat day after day, cancelling everything which might take him outside. He was in the bath when the call came. His extremely beautiful girlfriend – who knew nothing of motorsport – answered the phone and said it was someone called Tyrrell. Cevert sprang from the bath and, naked, grabbed the receiver from her . . .

He made his début in Holland and would never drive for anyone else in Grand Prix racing. Tyrrell, eyeing him paternally, said as Cevert prepared for practice: 'I have only one worry concerning François, that he wants to go too fast too soon. From our meetings I have gained the impression that he was impatient and wanted to impose himself quickly. I have therefore decided, from the start, to restrain him severly.'

Cevert's initial foray in the car confirmed all Tyrrell's suspicions. 'I found he was going too fast for the experience he had. "Finished for today," I told him early in the afternoon. He was very disappointed.' The next day, Tyrrell ordered Cevert to forget about doing a fast time – 'Jackie will help you later' – and instead, 'become familiar with the car, with its reactions.'

Stewart finished the race second, Cevert retired after 31 laps (a connecting rod problem). Tyrrell had been mistaken about Cevert in the sense that Cevert was prepared to learn rather than set all the tracks of the world on fire; and in Stewart he had the perfect teacher.

In the background, Tyrrell had hired a designer, Derek Gardner. In complete secrecy, Gardner designed the first Tyrrell, had a mock-up done and then the car itself was built at the factory. It was unveiled in August to general astonishment.

In 1971, armed with Gardner's car, Tyrrell changed from Dunlop to Goodyear tyres. Bert Baldwin worked for Goodyear and became close to the team. He remembers the discussions in Canada about the changeover. He'd find Tyrrell 'a great, great bloke. He was so direct, was Ken.

'Kyalami in 1971, our first season with the team, was very important in order to establish our best compound and construction set-up for the car. Prior to their change to Goodyear the car had been set up on Dunlop so we used a set of Dunlops to give it a base line. This testing was done in intense heat so it was first of all to find the best compound to give a ten-lap consistent run. Once we'd done this we ran through a series of constructions to blend with the particular car characteristics. Then we went through the compounds to find the one which would give a quick lap for qualification. We were also testing with other teams, of course.

'Ken always treated his staff and ourselves in the same manner: he was very demanding but also very appreciative of the support given to the team. And it wasn't all work and no play. For instance, in the evening we'd all go round to South African residents we knew – people like Paddy Driver[5] and Mike Hailwood – for a barbecue, a swim or a tennis match.'

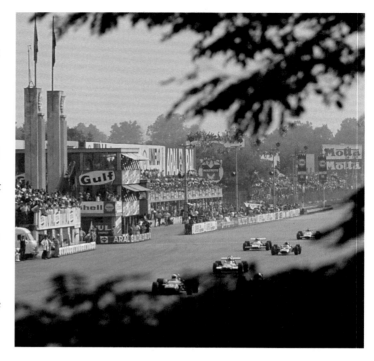

As Baldwin got closer to the team, this is what he found:

'During the race week at Kyalami we would play tennis at the Kyalami Ranch[6], Ken and Jackie vs Ed Alexander, my boss at Racing Division, and I. Believe it or not, we met on the court at 6am. Ken and Jackie invariably won, but we all thoroughly enjoyed the competitive games.

'The atmosphere in the team was fantastic. In testing at Kyalami the car might break down halfway round the circuit. Ken would send Roger Hill, his chief mechanic – a tall, gaunt lad – he'd say: "Go on, go and get the car back," and then to me "I'll tell you this: whatever tool he needs to get the car back he'll have in his pocket." Ken had so much faith in his personnel. It was a family concern and the personnel were part of that family. And it was a family concern right through the whole working team.

'I remember when Jackie brought the car in and I was working on the right front tyre. Jackie was all right when everything was all right and it may be that he wasn't happy about his own performance this day. Jackie looked at me and said: "You've no right to be smiling." Ken overheard this and looked at Jackie. "Your job is bloody racing and driving. You don't say things like that to people trying to help you." Jackie was controlled by Ken, there's no doubt about that.'

Another Goodyear employee, Graham Ball, got close, too, and was there for Stewart's 1971 championship. 'Ken? He was a super guy. He'd grab you by the shoulders, take you over to one side and give you a few home truths. He was a father figure, a gentleman and a figurehead – he'd have been that in any era. The team was a pretty good bunch of people. Ken wasn't the best of diplomats at times, I suppose, and he was there at the right time, before sponsorship was totally necessary. The whole atmosphere was completely different: motor racing has progressed and masses of money have come in to it.

'We used to go to Kyalami testing before the season began and we'd be there a month. Stewart had a brake failure at the end of the straight past the pits and I remember the whole car being wrapped up in the catch fencing with Stewart inside it. Fortunately it didn't catch fire and they got him out after a few minutes. Ken was very concerned about anything on the safety side . . .'

Stewart was as dominant in 1971 as he had been in 1969, second in South Africa, winning Spain, Monaco, France (Cevert second), Britain, Germany (Cevert second), Canada while Cevert won in the USA. Stewart had the championship with 62 points, Ronnie Peterson (March) next on 33 and Cevert third on 26.

Because Stewart's championships have been so well documented for so long, not least by Stewart himself, it is easy to view them simply as historical fact and move on. That forgets the romance of the racing before everything was money and vested interest, and it forgets the danger. Stewart once told me that in dark moments he imagined a vast dinner party for the drivers he'd known well, but only he and Helen went. All the others were dead.

It is equally easy to forget that Stewart was somewhere between pop idol, fashion icon [long hair, trendy then and slightly outrageous], very modern man, technocrat and genuine hero – and this at a time when Britain was in decline. The Tyrrell team and Stewart were the opposite of that: world beaters. That is what the championships really meant.

I wondered if there was another Ken Tyrrell that the outside world didn't see. 'I never saw one,' Stewart replied. 'He was the man to be with – even though he was very obstinate . . .'

Stewart's son Mark saw how close his father and Tyrrell were 'and no contract between them. It was a relationship, a friendship and an understanding: you do your job, I'll do mine and in that way we'll do it together. We'll communicate via that and get on with the task in hand rather than getting messed up with this, that and the other.'

This worked well enough to make Tyrrell the best team and Stewart thrice World Champion.

Bert Baldwin says that Tyrrell 'always invited us to the Christmas party and we'd drive down to Ockham. He had it at a really nice place and to me it was a really nice gesture. He had all the mechanics and their wives there, of course. Jackie's first championship [with Goodyear] he – Jackie – gave both Graham and I a signed Rolex watch at that party. It's that sort of thing that brings them back to being human.'

Reflecting, Baldwin and I agree that neither Tyrrell nor Stewart ever departed from being human, and so had no reason to be brought back – but you know what he means.

The 1972 season was more difficult, Stewart second in the championship to Emerson Fittipaldi (Lotus), Cevert joint sixth. Grand Prix racing, too, was enlarging itself. 'I stopped going racing because we were getting bigger and bigger and we had more and more employees,' Neil Davis says. 'Ken asked me to look after the factory, so I was factory manager to the end.'

Towards mid-season, Tyrrell's French connection would be reinforced. Patrick Depailler had had, at the age of 28, a varied career in motor racing with the highlight a victory in the Formula 3 race at the Monaco Grand Prix this year of 1972. Ken Tyrrell always noticed and noted things like that.

Depailler was driving a Renault Alpine and, one day in the spring, their press chief informed him that he would be driving a Tyrrell in the Grand Prix of France.

'I was stunned, I didn't believe my ears, I asked him to repeat it,' Depailler would remember[7]. 'In a single moment, I understood that the dream which I had been following for so many years was on the point of being realised. In a little more than two months, if my informer had told the truth, it would happen. But was it true? Ken Tyrrell I didn't really know at all, I'd scarcely even said "good-day" to him more than a couple of times. Without doubt he'd watched me.'

Strings, Depailler concluded, had been firmly pulled. However, 'I had so much fear that the reality would break the dream I didn't dare speak to François Guiter about it. It wasn't until a month later that he confirmed to me the good news. I was going to make my début in Formula 1 and, overjoyed with happiness, at home, at Clermont-Ferrand on the same track where exactly eight years earlier I had made my racing début.'

Spain, second race of the 1971 season, and Stewart wins from Ickx in the Ferrari (Sutton).

A curious relationship was born there, between Ken Tyrrell – externally so gruff but genial amidst the guffaws – and Depailler, externally so French but inwardly so introspective, quiet, perhaps even uncertain. Formula 1 breeds curious partnerships, but not many on quite this scale.

At Clermont-Ferrand before practice Depailler found himself struck dumb, the scale of the thing crowding him, as he listened to Tyrrell telling him: 'You know, Formula 1, it's very hard, nothing like what you have known up to here. It's so much more competitive. You are going to take part in your first Grand Prix. It is necessary for you to know that you have nothing to prove. Anyway, you have no chance of winning. I absolutely want that you drive within yourself, without taking any risks.'

With those words lingering in his ears, Depailler ventured out on to the track. As soon as he began to drive he felt much less intimidated by the car than by Tyrrell himself. However modest, Depailler was a racer. In first practice on the Friday he was 12th, 15th in the first on the Saturday and 19th in the afternoon. All that translated to the eighth row (of 12) – and he'd gone faster than Carlos Reutemann (Brabham), Graham Hill (Brabham) and a young Niki Lauda (March). *Autosport* concluded that he had 'far from disgraced himself.'

After qualifying 'I went home on the Saturday evening with the conviction that I could give a good performance. Tyrrell had told me that I had nothing to prove: we'd see about that . . .'

He was running at the end, five laps behind the winner (Stewart). He'd had to pit for a puncture.

Years later, Tyrrell would say 'I believed in him in 1972, when I gave him his first chance in Formula 1[8]. When I look today at the grid for that race I notice that Patrick qualified faster than Niki Lauda at the wheel of a factory March, as well as Graham Hill and Carlos Reutemann who drove the official Brabhams. Unfortunately, two stops at the pits prevented him from getting a good result, but it was clear the talent was there. Patrick drove for me again at the US Grand Prix that same year, qualified brilliantly again, and finished seventh. The following season, I had forseen running him in the USA again but before that he fell off a

motor bike and broke his leg. This accident didn't have any bearing on our future relationship, although there is a clause in his contract that while he drives for me he doesn't ride motor bikes any more!'

That was the future.

The 1973 season gave Stewart his third and final championship with Cevert now so accomplished that he was ready to assume Stewart's position. As Stewart says, 'I was going to retire anyway. That had already been decided with Ken earlier in the year. Cevert was poised to take over, he would have been the transition. In those days there was a Number 2 and a Number 1 and in 1974 he would have become Number 1.'

This is how the season unfolded, and this is how Cevert was positioning himself as the next Number 1: Cevert was second in Argentina and Stewart third; Stewart second in Brazil (Cevert unplaced); Stewart won South Africa (Cevert not classified); Cevert was second in Spain (Stewart did not finish, broken brake disc); Stewart won Belgium from Cevert; Stewart won Monaco, Cevert fourth; Cevert was third in Sweden, Stewart fifth; Cevert was second in France, Stewart fourth; Cevert was fifth in Britain, Stewart tenth; and that brought them to Holland and a revealing anecdote from Bert Baldwin.

'We had a situation at Zandvoort where Colin Chapman talked me into letting him have one set of used tyres for qualifying which were obviously better[9]. At midday, Chapman said: "Just let me have a used set, because it's not really fair." I said: "We can't do that," but eventually he talked me into doing it. Ronnie got pole. After that, Ken's eyes stood out like organ stops. He was really, really upset with me. Did he let me know? Oh, positively. I was really in the dog house . . .'

Stewart won Holland from Cevert; Stewart won Germany from Cevert; Stewart was second in Austria (Cevert crashed); and that brought them to Italy, where Stewart could take the championship. The opposition was from Lotus, Emerson Fittipaldi and Ronnie Peterson, but Stewart only needed to finish fourth provided Fittipaldi didn't win.

Stewart had qualified on the third row of the grid and

Jackie Stewart in Austria, 1971, but eventually the drive shaft failed and a wheel came off (Phipps/ Sutton). The core of the Tyrrell team, right – designer Derek Gardner, Tyrrell himself, Stewart and Cevert – pose with the Goodyear team at Monza, 1971. The championship had been won at the race before, Austria (Bert Baldwin).

ran fourth for the opening seven laps although the car was beginning to behave erratically. He could see a rear tyre deflating and had to pit. It was not a smooth stop and he emerged 20th, and this on the easy racetrack: it is true that in 1973 there were two chicanes (which *Autosport* described as 'silly' and 'narrow') but the rest of the 3.5m/ 5.7km essentially offered and rewarded top speed. What Stewart had done was stay on the same lap and he now began a sustained recovery which prompted Tyrrell to say some of the laps were 'incredible'. The race was 55 laps and by half distance Stewart was up to ninth. He could, and did, make up places at the first chicane, outbraking slower cars.

Opposite (clockwise from top left): Spain, 1973, where Cevert would finish second to the Lotus of Emerson Fittipaldi. A broken brake disc halted Stewart (Schlegelmilch). Cevert, on his way to fifth at the 1973 Italian Grand Prix, one place behind Stewart (Phipps/ Sutton). Stewart closing in on his third and final World Championship (Phipps/Sutton). Monza, the decisive race of 1973, and the Italians wanted to see it badly (Phipps/ Sutton).

From ninth, he overtook Ickx (Ferrari) whose engine was overheating, gained on and caught Mike Hailwood (Team Surtees), who had thumped a wheel against one of the chicane barriers – sixth – and, six laps later, passed Carlos Reutemann (Brabham) – fifth – to be behind Cevert. In seven laps he had caught Cevert who, deferring to the situation and Stewart's senority, moved across and let him through. Peter Revson (McLaren) lay ahead and, chasing him hard, Stewart bettered the lap record on lap 51 with 1m 35.3s (218kmh/ 135mph). Revson was too far away to be caught but that wasn't the story. Peterson led Fittipaldi and, instead of showing the deference which Cevert had, stayed in the lead to the end. Stewart had his third World Championship.

'Probably the best race I did for Ken was the Nürburgring in 1968 but winning the World Championship in Monza was pretty good coming up through the field because it was an easy racetrack; so much more difficult to find time there than it was at the Nürburgring, where I had 187 corners to choose from,' Stewart says. 'These two races were the best.'

He was fifth in Canada (Cevert crashed with a young South African, Jody Scheckter). The last race was the United States at Watkins Glen and in Saturday morning practice Cevert crashed with terrifying ferocity. He was killed instantly.

Stewart never drove again.

A decade after Stewart retired and Cevert died, I was interviewing Tyrrell at his home and the questions and answers moved along at a lively pace, as they were apt to do. Near the end, I asked him what the best and worst moments had been. I can't remember what the best was, but when he'd recounted it he murmured, 'the worst?' and, the voice lower, 'Cevert'. He looked away then, looked away just as he did at The Barley Mow that day a decade on from the interview when he recounted the story of Kenneth saying hello to Norah on the way back from Australia. Both times, he was very close to tears.

NOTES:
[1] Montlhéry, a banked circuit south of Paris.
[2] *Autosport.*
[3] *World Champion* by Jackie Stewart and Eric Dymock (Pelham Books, 1970).
[4] *François Cevert: la mort dans mon contrat.*
[5] Paddy Driver, a South African who was an accomplished bike rider and great friend of Mike Hailwood. He competed in a couple of South African car Grands Prix.
[6] Kyalami Ranch was a country hotel near the circuit where the drivers stayed.
[7] *Depailler* by Rosinski.
[8] *Ibid.*
[9] This story needs amplifying. Baldwin explains that Goodyear were using a different compound in the morning and these proved to be good tyres. They would be running a different compound in the afternoon qualifying. Emerson Fittipaldi had had some problem in the morning and hadn't been able to exploit his tyres. Chapman said this wasn't fair to Emmo, contractually Chapman had to give Emmo and Ronnie equal treatment – and he persuaded Baldwin to let him have a used set of the morning tyres for the afternoon. Finally, Baldwin agreed – and Chapman gave them to Peterson, who took pole! I imagine the whole paddock got a froth job when Tyrrell heard.

Chapter Four

FRANÇOIS

'He never took a single step without measuring all the consequences.'

Patrick Depa

'I still send flowers to François's grave every single year c his mother only died in the last twelve months. Every yea we'd always get a letter from his mother because we sent flowers. François was very close to Ken.'

Sir Jackie Stev

'Stewart was No. 1, no question about it, with Cevert fas coming up at No. 2. Beyond that I never saw anyone tha would have said was approaching them – although of co other people won races.'

Derek Gar

To assess the impact of Cevert's loss is as difficult no as it was then. You can certainly construct a case th in terms of winning world champioships the Tyrrell team never fully recovered. From the moment Cevert crashed the end in 1998, Tyrrell took only two more pole positic and won only seven more races. Jody Scheckter, who car in with Patrick Depailler in 1974, finished third in the championship and third again in 1976, but nowhere nea the championship itself. Tyrrell never were near again.

Part of the impact was obviously personal to Ken Ty 'I think,' Bob says, 'dad considered giving up.'

Part of the impact was that Cevert had been delibera groomed to take over as No. 1 when Stewart retired, wi either Scheckter or Depailler coming in as No. 2 – to be groomed in their turn. Now the succession was destroye

Bob points out that 'before Cevert drove for us he wa taking part in the Elf driving school. Dad was a judge.' other words, Tyrrell was there virtually at the beginning Later 'I was in Spain, because I studied Spanish at unive

The master and the pupil, Holland, 1970 (Schlegelmilch).

arcelona. Somehow I ended up with Cevert and his
r driving with whatever Formula 3 car he had on the
k of a trailer to another race. They must have been
ng me a lift. So we had got to know him a little bit,
ably through Guiter. "I think this guy's good," Guiter
t have said, and so on.

Cevert was just wonderful fun. He was flambuoyant.
 wanted to be a concert pianist and his parents were
t upset when he decided to pack that in and become a
ng driver. He had these wonderful big eyes, big blue eyes.
was a bit like Jean-Claude Killy in looks – or Sacha
el. He was of that ilk. Incidentally, it wasn't announced
Stewart was retiring and Jackie didn't even tell Helen
use he didn't want her counting the number of races to
n he stopped. People got killed in those days, regularly.
Then you'd got two new drivers coming in and the
tional problems that dad had of getting it all together
Cevert died as well. I think that was difficult, I think
ound that hard.' Nor can it have helped that the cause
evert's death was not known. 'If it had happened today
 have known what went wrong with the car, because
can find out. You didn't know in those days unless
 was something obvious, and even then you might not
use you didn't have telemetry.[1] Several drivers who
 for Tyrrell have died, but Cevert was the only one
 died in a Tyrrell.'

ackie Stewart insists that 'Cevert was very happy for
o teach him and if he hadn't had the accident either
iller or Scheckter would have come in as No. 2.
We were all a little bit like that about François, all of
When you see Mark's film, it's so strong.[2] It's very, very
ional. I can't watch it. Bellof hit Ken[3] very hard, too.
vent together to Crystal Palace to see François [in
] and Ken chose him. He was more like a young
ing cock. He was totally unaffected and yet so
dent and so sure of himself – although not because he
ght he was the best, because he actually never did
 that. He had a superb physique for a man. He had
enormous charm, such good manners, he was such a
nable individual who became a great friend of Ken
Norah, a great friend of Helen and I. He became part

of our family. There was a closeness between two team-
mates which probably would never occur today.

'There was a film that Elf made, *The Professor and The
Student*, and it was a whole year of François learning from
me[4] in French and it was very good. I kept telling Ken how
ready he was [in 1973] and I said on several occasions: "If I
don't win he is going to – he might be able to pass me." In
fact he was very respectful, I had the experience and I didn't
go to the edge when it wasn't necessary. All of these things
were beginning to come to François: that you didn't have to
go fast all the time, and at places like the Nürburgring he'd
started to challenge me. That gave me satisfaction.

'That's why to this day it has a tremendous effect on us.
I still send flowers to François's grave every single year and
his mother only died in the last twelve months. Every year
we'd always get a letter from his mother because we sent
the flowers. François was very close to Ken.'

Derek Gardner sets it all in context. 'Stewart was
arguably the best driver in his day. There was a wide
variation of cars: some smaller, more compact, narrower
and so on. Some were obviously easier to drive than others
but when it really came down to it there were very few of
the very quick combinations of good car, good driver. And
Stewart was No. 1, no question about it with Cevert fast
coming up at No. 2. Beyond that I never saw anyone that I
would have said was approaching them – although of
course other people won races.

'In my experience – and this goes back 25, 30 years – if
you have a mediocre car you will not get good results. That
has been proved umpteen times. I'm thinking now of
1970-73. Certainly in 1971 there was quite a number of
mediocre cars and some very good drivers. If you have a
mediocre car and a very good driver, the driver is going to
give the best performance of that marque but it isn't
necessarily going to win races. On the other hand you can
have very good motor cars and mediocre drivers and . . .
well, you have to be capable of seeing past all the glitz and
glamour, don't you?

'Now take JYS. He excelled at the Nürburgring, the old
Ring. In fact for lesser mortals like me it was terrifying.
Cevert had tremendous talent and the best was that he

Clockwise:
The happy
times (Bert
Baldwin).
François Cevert
at Watkins Glen,
October 1973
(Phipps/Sutton).

Possibly the last
picture of Cevert
and Tyrrell
together (Phipps/
Sutton). Stewart
facing the press at
Watkins Glen
(Phipps/Sutton).

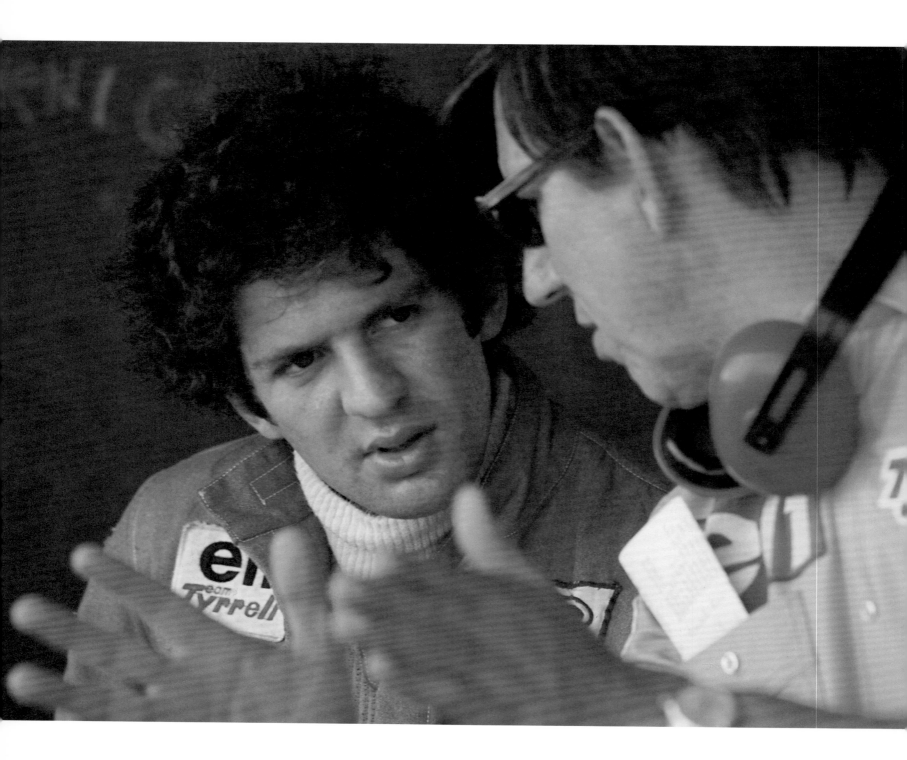

Opposite: The South African Jody Scheckter came into the team in 1974. Scheckter was intense and Ken Tyrrell could be too (Schlegelmilch). This page: Scheckter wins the 1974 Swedish Grand Prix from his team-mate Patrick Depailler (both Schlegelmilch).

looked upon Jackie as learning from the master. Stewart was quite content for that to happen, but inevitably the pupil goes on and goes on and gets better and better. In 1973 Cevert was very, very good indeed. Of course . . . it would have moved smoothly from one to the other, but it was not to be.'

How did you take that?

'We had a very good relationship, let me put it that way.'

So Scheckter came and Depailler came; and whereas Cevert had seen Tyrrell's benign, paternal face, Depailler saw a different one. He would write this:[5]

'I had arrived just as a crossroads had been reached [by the team] and that's what made my début there very difficult. Until then, Ken had lived in the certainty that it was the driver who constituted the most important factor in a championship. And it was true. It was – truly – Stewart more than Tyrrell who must be credited with winning the title in 1973. I know this, because I drove that car in 1974 and I know that it was nothing exceptional. The 1974 season marked the beginning of Ferrari's supremacy and from that moment on all the teams had to redouble their efforts on the technical side to succeed.

'At first Ken didn't understand. I am sure that Stewart would not have been World Champion in 1974 with the material we had, Jody and I. It had become impossible – but Ken still believed it. Then, instead of taking us into his confidence step by step, he psychologically disarmed us by knocking us, by leading us a hard life. He believed it was character forming. In reality, it complicated our relationships.

'It was me who suffered the most because I had difficulty expressing myself in English, and also because my timidity stopped me from taking a lead. It's why I was behind compared to Scheckter – but Jody had a hard time, too, and I am sure that it's because he took this badly that he decided to go.

'Ken is an intelligent man and since then he has changed a lot. He has understood that he must revise his approach, re-examine his methods. Today [1978] he doesn't attribute sole responsibility for set-backs to his drivers, he interests himself in the mistakes by his technicians. I know it when I see how he treats Pironi [we'll be coming to Didier Pironi in due course]. He, like me, had to integrate into the team, learn how to understand. He will certainly take less time than I did because he speaks good English – but overall because Tyrrell has changed. Now, when we analyse the races to come, he doesn't treat us like irresponsible youngsters.

'For two years, our relationship was so uneasy that at the end of the 1975 season I had lost confidence. He didn't want me anymore, we didn't understand each other anymore, we didn't reach out to communicate anymore. We had arrived at the point where we weren't working together.

'Our cars weren't on the pace. Jody went faster than me sometimes. I was blocked, I had lost morale and I was dragging along. Ken told me, and repeated, that I was no good. I replied: "It's the car which is no good." He did not yet accept the fact that the cars were slow, and I was incapable of prevaling over him. Then there was a click: he had understood. Ever since, the tyrant is dead.

'If sometimes I detested him, I sincerely admire Ken. He is a fascinating man, endowed with an enormous personality. He is the opposite of me and yet at the same time he complements me. I am impulsive, sometimes I have a tendency to get carried away. With the systematic rigour that he brings to bear in everything, he obliged me to temper my judgements, he stopped me from making mistakes. He never took a single step without measuring all the consequences.

'Now that we know each other well, we accept each other as we are and we have worked out our system of co-operation: I take him all the information I can gather and he sifts it. In sum, he counterbalances me.'

Tyrrell, contributing a foreword to Depailler's book, wrote: 'I can easily imagine that Patrick will explain to you that things weren't easy for him, and among those things the least easy of all was . . . Ken Tyrrell! Anyway, that's what he said ceaselessly to me during the five years that he has driven for me. According to the norms established in the Formula 1 teams our partnership is already ancient and I like to

Depailler rides The Ring in 1974, before being halted by a suspension problem . . . Scheckter won the 1974 British Grand Prix at Brands Hatch and Tyrrell joined the fun on the podium (both Schlegelmilch).

think that Patrick now considers himself a member of the Tyrrell family. We don't always agree and Patrick will surely confirm that, but I think we do good work together.

'Patrick hasn't an impressive physique but he becomes a tiger when he gets behind the wheel of a racing car. He practises to the ultimate and that's one of the essential reasons why I have kept him in the team for five years. I am writing these words at the beginning of the 1978 season and Patrick is still waiting for his first victory – me too! However, he has had second and third places which were worth victories. He has amply demonstrated that he possesses the determination and talent of a winner. And the fact that Patrick doesn't allow himself to be discouraged by the apparent ill luck which fate has thrown at him is to his credit.'

An aside from Tyrrell: 'I particularly remember the 1975 German Grand Prix, where Patrick had a fantastic duel with Niki Lauda. Lap after lap they came past the pits wheel-to-wheel before disappearing in the diabolical meanderings of the Nürburgring. That day Patrick was affirmed as the equal of the driver who would become World Champion at the end of the season. Alas, the suspension broke and Patrick was forced to come back to the pits slowly. He had lost a race but won the admiration of everyone.'

Scheckter saw this other aspect of Tyrrell, too. 'He approached me to drive for him when Jackie was retiring. It was, if I remember, Watkins Glen. I didn't have to impress – I knew – that he was the team to be with. There wasn't much question about it. How did I find him? Let's talk about the things that stood out. First of all the way he looked after Norah was a lesson in my life. I will always remember having meetings in Brazil. The car was terrible, you felt like killing everybody around you and he'd stop in the middle of a technical meeting to make sure that Norah could get home all right! That aggravated me so much, but it gave me an understanding that from a human point of view Ken was such a lovely guy.

'I think a lot of mistakes were made in the process of Ken and myself – or that era, should I say, not Ken and myself. Saying that we weren't as good as Jackie Stewart, well, fine, you know. But they deliberately tried to build a car that was much easier to drive rather than a car that was going to be fast, and I think that that was the start of things going wrong. They felt they had two young guys and so they approached it in a different way. It was my first full year in Grand Prix racing and I had to develop the car with Patrick Depailler, who was also inexperienced. They didn't really want to believe what you said, they always wanted to tell you how Jackie Stewart did it and maybe if Jackie had been there I could have learnt a lot – but he wasn't there. And don't forget we could have won the championship in 1974. We left Italy equal leading the championship and then the brakes broke and, OK, we landed up third.

'I found the team to be not very technical. McLaren had moved the wing back and that was the big tweak in those days – and we hadn't. On our Formula 5000 cars we had done it a year before. They were still running the wing close. I think they were sliding back at that stage.'

Scheckter finished third in the 1974 championship and Depailler ninth; a year later Scheckter was joint seventh and Depailler ninth again. The team seemed to be going nowhere in particular. Derek Gardner was already working on changing all that and what he'd do astonished everyone, starting with Scheckter and Depailler themselves. A sense of wonder and a measure of controversy lingers over it still, a quarter of a century on.

Notes:
[1] Computers monitor every function of a racing car to extraordinary detail and precision.
[2] *Ken Tyrrell, Surviving Formula 1.*
[3] Stefan Bellof, a young German of great flair and daring, was killed in a sportscar race at Spa in August 1985. He was combining the sportscars with Formula 1 for Tyrrell, and was in the middle of his second season with the team.
[4] Stewart is not bragging (he's not like that, anyway) about speaking French. He lived in the French-speaking part of Switzerland and once, when he telephoned for a taxi to take me from his house to the railway station, he did so in a surprisingly fluent way.

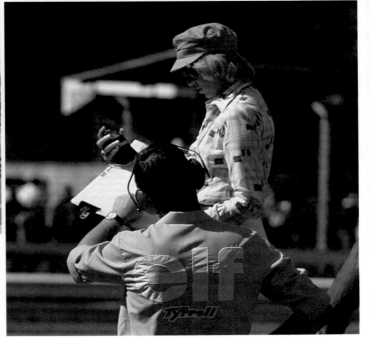

Scheckter at the 1975 Austrian Grand Prix, where he'd finish eighth. (Schlegelmilch)

... Tyrrell and Depailler confer, Germany, 1975 (Schlegelmilch).

... Norah, mistress of Monza (Phipps/Sutton).

Chapter Five

SIX INTO FOUR WON'T GO

'A racing car is a wonderful thing, gifted with life. A new racing car is a child which has just been born, which you have to teach to walk, to read, to write, which must be preserved from danger because it is fragile, awkward, naïve.'
Patrick Depailler

'Well, in those days we operated a very simple principle, and it's still the most reliable: if you don't want people to know, you don't tell them!'
Derek Gardner

'The initial impression is like being in a bobsleigh – that lasts two laps then you know where it's going.'
Martin Stretton

The world was a more restrained, more measured place then. In September 1975, Tyrrell unveiled their car for 1976 at the Heathrow Hotel, London Airport. It was done with a certain sense of theatre, the car covered while Stewart, Tyrrell and Gardner made speeches. Then the veil was drawn off and the assembled journalists saw it. There seems to have been a moment of complete disbelief: a racing car with six wheels. It was a concept so radical that even now disbelief is not difficult to summon. *Autosport* called it 'sensational' and for once the word seemed justified. And yet, on the front cover of the magazine two NASCAR racers were pictured and a small headline across the top of the page said only

Peterson battled to sixth at Monza in 1977, one of only three points finishes that season (Schlegelmilch).

'NEW TYRRELL AND LOTUS GRAND PRIX CARS'. The Tyrrell did not appear until page 10.

There's a lovely anecdote from Neil Davis, the Tyrrell employee: 'Denis Jenkinson[1] rang Ken and said he could not make it the day it was being unveiled because he had a prior engagement. Ken in his little devious way – because he loved Jenkinson, loved winding him up – said: "Well, Denis, I'll tell you what we'll do. We'll give you a preview provided you do not write or say anything until the following day." Jenkinson said: "Yes, I'll do that, Ken." So we took the six-wheeler up to Ken's house and Jenkinson was gobsmacked, wasn't he? He couldn't believe his eyes. I don't think we could when it was first decided to make one!'

Eoin Young had a hand in this (he was handling the press releases). 'I invited Jenks for a sneak preview. The photos of the six-wheeler were taken on Tyrrell's lawn at home. Jenks walked round the corner of the house, stopped in his tracks and hurried back around the corner saying he was obviously hallucinating: he'd just seen a racing car with six wheels. He added that when he came round the corner again he'd find it was either gone or restored to four!'

The press release and the accompanying photograph (Bert Baldwin).

At the unveiling, Tyrrell 'cheerfully' admitted that the car had not turned a wheel. Some journalists were openly sceptical that it ever would.

The car was tested in March and – restrained – *Autosport* carried a teasing story of only two paragraphs the week before, under a small heading, 'SIX-WHEEL ON'. It began: 'As we confidently expected, Elf Team Tyrrell are going ahead with plans to race their exciting six-wheel Grand Prix car (Project 34).'

Now, recording the test – at Silverstone – *Autosport* hoisted up a headline which was only slightly larger: 'SIX-WHEEL F1 CHALLENGE'. It began: 'Following a concentrated programme of development over the winter . . .' and pointed out that the engineer who conceived it, Derek Gardner, felt the car so radical that it was 'beyond the theme of his conventional double-zero cars which began with the 001 model for Jackie Stewart in 1970.' Hence Project 34.

Patrick Depailler was the first to drive it and did a 'scintillating' time of 1m 18.2, a mere 0.1 seconds slower that the fastest test time at Silverstone so far that season. As Depailler brought the car down the straight at racing speed Gardner watched 'horrified' – his word. We'll reach that in a moment.

Tyrrell confirmed that he intended to run the car in the Spanish Grand Prix at Jarama on 2 May and hoped to have one each for Scheckter and Depailler. The story behind the car is almost as amazing as the car itself.

'The concept really went back to the Lotus turbine car – I was responsible for the four-wheel-drive part of that car,' Gardner says.[2] 'In those dark days – dark, in terms of enlightenment – the actual behaviour of four-wheel drive cars wasn't very well known. Consequently, when you took it to a particular track, like Indianapolis, the change in characteristics caused the car to be particularly nervous.

'I wasn't really in a position to say: "Look, you've got it all wrong." How could I? I was a transmission engineer, against arguably the finest chassis constructor of all time, after all [Colin Chapman]. By the end of 1968 I was a good deal stronger in my views and I thought "Well, what we really want here is an entirely different concept". I thought about it, and came up with a drawing which was for a six-wheel car, four at the front, two at the rear – with two of the four front wheels being driven, plus the two at the rear. And as I developed the idea, I could see that one could reduce the size of the wheels, that you could actually narrow the track,[3] should you so wish, and all sorts of glorious things.

'So, by the end of 1968, I thought: "I'll put a proposal, privately, to Andy Granatelli."[4] I sent a long letter, and a drawing, suggesting how this could all be done. What I didn't know was that Granatelli was again locked in mortal combat with USAC, who didn't really understand why the turbine cars had gone quickly, and thought that if they banned turbine engines and four-wheel-drive they could get back to their beloved roadsters!

'I never got a reply from Andy, I was pretty disgusted and I just filed the idea away. Many years later, faced with the fact that all the top cars had Ford engines – the only other one available was the Matra, and no one wanted

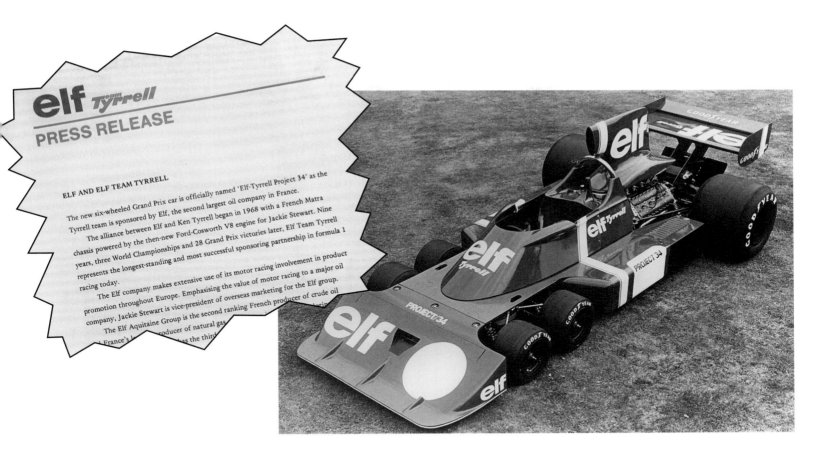

elf *Team Tyrrell*

PRESS RELEASE

ELF AND ELF TEAM TYRRELL

The new six-wheeled Grand Prix car is officially named 'Elf-Tyrrell Project 34' as the Tyrrell team is sponsored by Elf, the second largest oil company in France.

The alliance between Elf and Ken Tyrrell began in 1968 with a French Matra chassis powered by the then-new Ford-Cosworth V8 engine for Jackie Stewart. Nine years, three World Championships and 28 Grand Prix victories later, Elf Team Tyrrell represents the longest-standing and most successful sponsoring partnership in formula 1 racing today.

The Elf company makes extensive use of its motor racing involvement in product promotion throughout Europe. Emphasising the value of motor racing to a major oil company, Jackie Stewart is vice-president of overseas marketing for the Elf group.

The Elf Aquitaine Group is the second ranking French producer of crude oil France's la ... oducer of natural gas ... as the third

that because all the horsepower went down through the exhaust pipes, and no one wanted a BRM engine for much the same reasons! So I thought: "How on earth does one steal a march on the rest?" It seemed to me that really what we were looking for was another 50 horsepower, but how on earth were we going to get that – bearing in mind that I was associated with a man [Ken Tyrrell] for whom the Ford Motor Company was the only company in the world?

'I went searching through all my files, and came up with this proposal I'd sent to Granatelli. I did some calculations and came to the conclusion that if I had a car with four front wheels and two rear wheels, and the fronts could be contained within the 1,500mm at the front, I could reduce the amount of lift generated by normal front wheels, which would allow me to back off on the front aerodynamics – and, hey presto!, the figure I came up with was 40-odd horsepower.

'Eventually I showed it to Ken, who said: "Good grief!

What's this?" But actually it wasn't as difficult to sell him the idea as you might imagine. On the way back from the 1975 South African Grand Prix, I talked my way into First Class for a bit, in order to talk with Jackie Stewart about it. Now whether it was turbulence or something in his drink I don't know, but he had a fit of choking! He'd never seen anything like it before.

'I talked it over again with Ken, and said: "Well, first of all we've to find somebody who can make the tyres." We were contracted to Goodyear, so the next thing was a high-powered meeting with them. They didn't raise any eyebrows, they said yes, they'd support us. What size did we want? I said: "Well, ideally, I'd like nine-inch tyres" so we compromised – on 10!

'First of all, I designed the complete car, and then looked at it again to see how I could very quickly produce such a car. The upshot was that, from the roll-over bar forward, it was a new car but a very simple one – it was not a raceworthy car. The rear was straightforward 007,[5] just

bolted on. It really was a "bitza" [bits and pieces!] but of course it looked quite peculiar.

'To be absolutely precise, we equipped a conventional car with the four front wheels while leaving the rears as they were, mainly to see what we had. Yes it is difficult, but when you've lived with something for quite a long time it becomes easier. You have to accept compromises and allow for that. It would have started about 1974 but when it was first unveiled at one of the hotels in Heathrow the car had never turned a wheel. This was a proof of concept, let's put it that way, so the world now knew it was going to happen but they didn't know whether it was going to work or not. We had no doubts at all but the people who went along and looked at it were sharply divided into those who thought "Yes, it will work" and those who thought "No, can't possibly – otherwise it would have been done." You know all the arguments.

'Quite a few people took the mickey out of the idea. In fact, Eoin Young[6] compiled a book with all the quotations of the various people – and there were a lot of them – bearing in mind it had never turned a wheel on the track. It was amusing to see how, as the car was very successful, they managed to change their tune.' (In response, Young says 'I think that's one of those things I wish I had done, but didn't!')

'In those days we operated a very simple principle, and it's still the most reliable: if you don't want people to know, you don't tell them! Yes, the Goodyear people knew about it, but, you know, there was a lot of racing with Minis in those days, with people doing peculiar things with them, and they had small wheels – so perhaps that helped provide a bit of fog.'

Scheckter caught the wind, sensing that Tyrrell and Gardner had something 'strange' going on. This was reinforced because Tyrrell would almost tease him by asking if he would like a car with 20 per cent more grip at the front and other, similar questions. Scheckter, puzzled, speculated with Depailler about what it could all mean and, although their imaginations produced some 'weird' answers, a six-wheeler was not among them.

'We produced P34, which was very much the prototype.

It was purely a test vehicle, but it was weighted up to what I thought the race car would probably be,' Gardner says. 'The aerodynamics were fairly appalling, actually, so it didn't gain anything from that, but inherently it was quicker – turn-in and so on was all marvellous.'

Gardner had showed Scheckter and Depailler the blueprint.

Depailler said: 'Zut alors!' – which means 'you don't say!', and 'blimey!'

Scheckter said 'Jeez.'

'There was a problem with the tyres,' Gardner says. 'Because of the nature of the tyres – the actual construction – if you stiffened up the carcass in order to control the profile at high speed, you stiffened up the sidewall – you just couldn't separate them. If they'd been radial-ply you could have separated them, but they weren't.'

Graham Ball, then of Goodyear, explains the situation from the tyre point of view. 'There was a lot more freedom then. Today, even it were allowed, there's no way we'd make a six wheeler – no way Goodyear would turn round and say we're going to make a special tyre for one team. In the days when racing tyres were being produced in Wolverhampton, away from Goodyear's corporate headquarters in Akron, we had a lot more freedom and we were able to do these sorts of things.'

Ball also explains that 'on a cross-ply tyre the cord is at 35-40 , and goes from the bead right the way round to the other bead, and that forms the carcass. A radial tyre has a ply that goes from one bead straight across and then you have a breaker over the top and both are independent – so you can change either. At that time everybody was running cross-ply tyres.'

Gardner remembers that 'the first time I saw the car, coming down the straight at Silverstone, I was absolutely horrified because I could see the tyres literally being sucked off the rims with the speed. As soon as the driver touched the brakes, they just collapsed down on to the rim. In actual fact, they never lost any pressure. It was just one of those hair-raising things and fortunately the drivers couldn't see it!

Tyrrell with Derek Gardner, who designed the six-wheeler, and Patrick Depailler, who adored it . . . Depailler driving it . . . and the front wheels (all Phipps/Sutton).

'The second problem was with the front brake calipers: because of the smallness of the wheel, cooling the brakes was a problem. You could accept the temperature of the brakes, but what you couldn't do was get the temperature away from the fluid. Now these days of course we would force fluid through it like they do on touring car brakes. Those were the only real problems. Other than that, we'd just run it . . .'

Gardner's basic thinking was: 'One could take it as read that there was a reduction in drag [in the shape small front wheels allowed] and therefore one could go faster in a straight line. And, theoretically, it should have had enormous stopping power, but we were hampered there, as I say, by just getting the heat away from the brakes. It wouldn't be a problem today.'

Depailler would remember 'as soon as I was let in on the secret I was enthusiastic. I was then at the lowest point in my relationship with Tyrrell, but Ken also took note that my belief in the six-wheeler was as hard as iron, even though Scheckter manifested an unconcealed suspicion towards it. From that moment on, Ken changed his attitude to me and put more and more trust in me.'

Depailler would[7] 'never forget the first test, at Silverstone. I believe I have never felt an emotion like it. For me, a racing car is even more than a tool which will perhaps allow me to win races, money and fame. A racing car is a wonderful thing, gifted with life. And a new racing car which you are going to give its first laps, it's a child which has just been born, which you have to teach to walk, to read, to write, which must be preserved from danger because it is fragile, awkward, naïve. And also because when you think of the passionate people who have conceived and constructed this work of art, the gigantic work that they have accomplished, the love they have brought to it, you feel crushed by your responsibility to them. At the moment of starting the engine, I told myself that I could break everything, reduce to nothing these hours and hours of strenuous work, and I felt an impression of paralysis and exultation at the same time. As soon as I took the six wheels in my hands for the first time, I have never felt such sentiments with so much violence.'

Gardner says 'Patrick was the first driver to test the car, at Silverstone, and his immediate impression was that it was very, very, quick. He also said that it turned in beautifully. I think he was just over the moon with it. If anything, we had to keep a tight rein on him!'

Scheckter drove the car – also at Silverstone – shortly before the Spanish Grand Prix. He was an *Autosport* columnist and wrote that he didn't think Gardner 'would have been very pleased if he'd known my reaction' that first time.

'It was just like driving a saloon car. I couldn't see the front wheels. I couldn't aim at the apex of the corner, I had to judge it and move in bit by bit each lap until I touched the apex. Then I knew where I was. It really was just like driving a saloon again.

'The other strange feeling driving it for the first time was that it felt like driving a pair of roller skates. The second pair of front wheels felt as if they were right underneath me. It really was a very uncanny feeling.

'But despite these two differences it didn't take long to get the feel of the car and work myself into a revised technique to drive it. Strangely, the technique isn't radically different. I guess the easiest comparison for the everyday motorist would be that it's just like the change-over from driving a left-hand drive car to a right-hand drive model.

'Before I'd got used to the narrowness of the front end I was going into corners and discovering on the way out that I'd missed the apex by feet. Then, as I moved over and came closer to the apex next time around, I'd find that I was able to turn in later and on the exit I'd have room to spare. In other words the car was much more economical in terms of the amount of road it used going through a corner.

'And very simply that means one is scoring on two counts: first you're saving split tenths of a second going through the corner and secondly, because of the clean, economical line out, you're getting up to your maximum speed earlier.'[8]

Scheckter added: 'The other really interesting thing about the six-wheeler is people's reaction to it. When it was first shown to the press at the Elf reception there were sniggers, and people didn't know whether to laugh or applaud. The reaction with the drivers and team managers

Scheckter (3) finished second in the 1976 Monaco Grand Prix, and Depailler (4) third. It seemed that the six-wheeler really did work. There were still points to discuss though (all Schlegelmilch).

Clockwise from top left: Triumph in the race after Monaco, the 1976 Swedish Grand Prix. Scheckter won from Depailler (Phipps/Sutton) . . . Every pit board tells a story (Phipps/Sutton) . . . The deceptive podium at Anderstorp, Tyrrell 1 and 2, and the six-wheeler dominant. It never would be again (Phipps/Sutton) . . . Bert Baldwin working on the small front tyres in Goodyear's test bed in Luxembourg, which they could only use at night because of all Goodyear's commercial activities. He wrote a caption himself: '9.20pm, 30.12.75' (Bert Baldwin).

was much the same. They poked fun at it and were always pulling our leg about it. Now that we've run it, the drivers just try very hard to ignore it. And the team managers! Every time it turns a wheel they're over to the rail with a stopwatch in their hand like a bunch of startled jack rabbits.'

At Jarama, Depailler had the P34 and Scheckter the orthodox 007. Perhaps that reflected an undercurrent that while Depailler was lost in enthusiasm for the P34, Scheckter was much, much less so.

Depailler qualified it on the second row (1m 19.11s against James Hunt's McLaren, pole on 1m 18.52s) and was running third when, on lap 26, the brakes failed.

Depailler explained that 'it had happened once before, in testing. Suddenly you push the pedal and it goes to the floor. You can pump and get it back again but by this time it was too late and I spun.'

In Spain, Tyrrell described the six-wheeler as a 'child of the regulations.'

Autosport wrote: 'Bluntly, nobody was laughing any more. Ken Tyrrell was going round like a schoolboy with his first pit pass, a grin never absent from his face.'

Gardner explains that 'once you got above a certain temperature you just lost your brakes. We resolved the problem by just pushing more and more air through the brakes – which, of course, tended to be counter-productive on the aerodynamics. But we coped.'

In Belgium two weeks later, both drivers had the P34, Depailler putting his on the second row again, Scheckter on the fourth. Depailler's engine failed in the race (when he was fourth) but Scheckter finished fourth, albeit 1m 31s behind the winner, Lauda.

At Monaco two weeks after that, Depailler was quickest in the first of three practice sessions – from Scheckter – and they qualified on the second and third rows respectively. Lauda won again, from Scheckter (@ 11 seconds) and Depailler (@ 1m 04s).

Derek Gardner remembers Monaco. 'Depailler was very French, he was first on the scene with the six-wheeler and he found that you got a great deal of kudos out of it. The press were always around. Probably the best example of all this was when we were up at the crack of dawn and he drove it without its bodywork around the streets of Monte Carlo, giving a commentary in French such as only Patrick could do. He loved to do it, Elf wanted him to do it and he was a Frenchman in Monaco. Put it all together and what have you got? He went round very quickly, it had been raining, the track was slippy and he was giving this wonderful commentary and the car gets out of line at about the tunnel and his voice raises immediately – and then it vanished into the tunnel!'

In fact, observers like Nigel Roebuck felt that the great strength of the car was the way it went into corners and this was particularly apparent at somewhere like Monte Carlo.

'Yes,' Gardner says. 'Thinking back, what I'd like to have done was to refine those areas. It didn't need anything major, but what it did need was development work on the tyres themselves. Ideally, they should have been radial-ply.' That of course brought an obvious problem, because Goodyear were only making 10-inch tyres for Tyrrell. 'Well, if you recall, at that time Goodyear were looking after the entire F1 circus. Firestone had gone, so it really was an enormous task for Goodyear. People wanted development, so they tended to develop the rear tyres and the normal front tyres. Our front tyres just sort of got left, so we were dealing with developed rears and static fronts, and by 1977 that was beginning to show up, and the advantage of the six-wheel concept was going rapidly out of the window.'

That was the future. Now, in June 1976 Scheckter reflected[9]: 'We had proved that the six-wheeler works well on fast circuits like Brands Hatch and medium-fast circuits like Zolder, but the big question was would its advantages show on the world's most tortuous, twisty, demanding circuit. The answer, I'm delighted to say, was a resounding yes.'

Better, much better, was coming in Sweden. Scheckter took pole, Depailler on the second row although during the practice Scheckter actually lost one of the wheels – it broke off. Far from hurling him off the circuit, as a conventional car would have done, the P34 only felt 'spongy' and he motored back to the pits amazed at how stable the car was. He sat there, the car stationary, and even more amazing – nobody noticed what had happened. Gardner naturally came over, knelt beside the cockpit and asked Scheckter how it was going. Scheckter nodded: OK. Tyrrell came over and he and Scheckter chatted, again quite naturally. Scheckter, however, could barely hear what Tyrrell was saying because he was struggling so hard to keep a straight face. At last a mechanic noticed the missing wheel and assumed another mechanic must have already taken it off. Only when he looked again did he realise . . .

Mario Andretti (Lotus) led the race to lap 46 when his engine failed, and Scheckter assumed the lead, made no mistake and won it – from Depailler, 19.766 seconds behind.

Team talk at the 1976 French Grand Prix (top left), where Depailler was second (Phipps/Sutton) . . . For 1977, Scheckter left and Ronnie Peterson came in (Phipps/Sutton) . . . Peterson had been quick all his life, in everything, but didn't get on with the car and could finish the 1977 season with only seven points (Phipps/Sutton).

Bert Baldwin of Goodyear puts that into context. 'Sweden being a tight circuit, you didn't get that long, long straight. The big problem we had was the tyre's sidewall sucking in and deflating. That was the object of the exercise when we were testing at Luxembourg[10]: to find a tyre which would not suck in at the sidewalls. The machine we were using was an aircraft machine and we could race it at 200mph. But imagine a tyre at 200mph – the number of revolutions that that does in relation to the rear tyre is phenomenal. One turn of the rear wheel must be three turns of the front wheel. The tyres would deflate and I had to find a construction which wouldn't deflate. On a circuit, any straight took the life out of the tyres.'

That pole position was the last that the Tyrrell team ever had, although it contested virtually every race for another 22 seasons.

Gardner was not surprised that the P34 had proved fast immediately 'because all the testing we'd done on the prototype the year before. We'd read that across on to the new car and it worked out very well.'

Paradoxically, as we have seen, Depailler was more committed to the P34 than Scheckter, something Gardner confirms. 'Yes, he was. That's absolutely right. He seemed to take to it like a duck to water. Jody . . . well, you know, you'd see his head go on one side . . .

'He would drive it, but I know it wasn't with total commitment. For all that, though, he did win at Anderstorp, of course. Patrick was an absolutely committed racer. He loved racing cars – to be a racing driver was the only thing he had ever wanted to do. He liked everything about the P34. It was a great pity that he didn't have that last little indefinable bit that gives you the chequered flag – he was so near on so many occasions. He was an excellent driver, and very good to work with. Occasionally, he'd be a bit mercurial but he was a French racing driver, after all!'

Reflecting now, Scheckter says: 'I think then Derek Gardner got under too much pressure from himself, or whatever, to do something that was better than anybody else. It was in my opinion a lousy car and lousily put together. It broke all the time. In my opinion all the theories were wrong. I understood at the time that it was narrow, it had a smaller frontal area and it would brake better because it had six wheels – and it didn't.

'I didn't agree with the theories. Now immediately the problem with that was that I was the one they didn't like. You can understand that. They had done all this, launching secret designs, and it all took a massive amount of work – and I'm saying: "No, I don't think it's right" and Depailler is saying: "eet ees fantastic." So it landed up where, I suppose, I was the Number One driver and I was no longer the Number One driver, even though I was still doing better.'

Depailler finished second in France, Scheckter second in Britain, Scheckter second in Germany, neither finished in Austria, Scheckter was fifth in Holland, he was fifth and Depailler sixth in Italy, Depailler was second in Canada and Scheckter second in the USA. Depailler was second in Japan. Cumulatively this made Scheckter third in the Championship and Depailler fourth, which proved to be slightly deceptive. The six-wheeler was not the future and Scheckter had surely worked that out because he resigned from Tyrrell (to use the language of that time) in early September. He said: 'I think Derek Gardner is a little disappointed with it' – the six-wheeler. 'As yet, it hasn't done many of the things it was expected to do. It's only as good as a good four-wheeler and it's quite complicated to drive. But with more development

it will probably improve.' Reflecting now, Scheckter says: 'The last year wasn't that great. I don't remember much of it. And it was time to move on.'

Incidentally, Tyrrell was estimating that in 1976 it cost £800,000 a season to compete in the Grands Prix and two non-championship races but would reveal no more because 'I don't want my rivals to know how I can manage to do things so cheaply.'

He signed a Swede, Ronnie Peterson, and said he'd been trying to sign him since Stewart retired. (Peterson had been with Lotus since 1973). Tyrrell had 'no doubt in my mind that he is a potential world champion.' Moving into 1977 Tyrrell said: 'He always tries no matter how bad the car may be. In this line of business you have to accept that a team can be worse than another. Formerly I have also found unknown talents and developed them into top drivers, but I couldn't develop Ronnie. He's the best and he's been so for a long time. I can't teach him anything. In the first races we don't count on any results. It's not so easy to adapt from always having driven on four wheels to six.'[11]

In Brazil, the second race of 1977, Peterson crashed and the car was virtually destroyed. He said to Tyrrell: 'Ken, now that we're going to build a new car, couldn't we put a

little window so I could see the wheels? I'm sitting so low I can't see them. I've no idea where I've got the car. I always aim with the tyres at the corners, but now I can see nothing. It's very irritating.'

Gardner says 'the little side-windows we put in the cockpit sides were there to allow the drivers to see the tyres, to pick up the shadow across the tyres. Whatever you may have been told at the time, those windows were not put in to allow spectators to see the drivers' hands at work . . .'

By mid-season, it was obvious the six-wheeler was essentially doomed. After the British Grand Prix, Depailler had ten points, Peterson four – and this from a man expected to win races.

What went wrong? 'Well,' Gardner says, 'We were suffering from undeveloped rubber at the front . . . and that problem got worse and worse, to the point that I even hurriedly contrived a wide-track front, to try and conteract the problem. By then the writing was on the wall. Either something had to be done about the tyres, or we had to forget the whole thing. And, well, as you know, I departed after Monza[12].

'Over the winter of '76–'77 we'd spent a lot of time in the wind tunnel, developing as near an enveloping bodyshape as it was possible to do. At that time they were trying to get rid of airboxes, so we came up with a wonderful plenum chamber that was fed with tapering ducts to two NACA ducts at the front. It worked beautifully: very low drag. It gave pressure recovery into the engine. The body, although it was extremely heavy because it was made in fibreglass [no carbon fibre in those days], worked well. Of course, you needed a pit that was twice the width of an ordinary one, because when you took it off the car, where did you put it?! Of course it wouldn't be a problem today – but it was then. Later in the season we had Kevlar bodywork, and that made quite a difference. That was very early days for Kevlar. With all that, it should have been a whole lot different, but of course it all came down to the rubber.

'As time went on, through 1977, it was getting to an impossible situation. Other teams had appreciated we had something inherently superior, and they'd pulled all the stops out: cars were improving enormously in 1977. People were experimenting with fixed skirts, and all sorts of bits and pieces, and it was time to take stock.'

At one point, Tyrrell even reverted to 1976 cars – at Jarama, Depailler was a second slower than he'd been in 1976, when the car was brand-new. 'Yes, it's true. Again, in 1977, Patrick was far and away the more committed of the drivers, consistently so.

'This is not a criticism of Goodyear, but they supplied the tyres, you put them on and you had nothing to check them against. If other teams had been using them, you'd have soon been saying: 'Well, this isn't working for us – is it working for you? We were trying to push Goodyear along, and not so gently! We were talking to them, saying "look, you've got to do something." The only thing on the horizon was the gentlemen from Clermont-Ferrand [Michelin]. We used to choose our tyres so that you could get the circumference within . . . well, if you were within five or six millimetres, you were doing very well. Sometimes, it was a heck of a lot more than that. You could pick up a Michelin tyre, spin it, and it was as if you'd turned it out of a solid lump of rubber.

'I think this reflected the enormous work load that Goodyear had, but we paid the heaviest price, no question

about that. Their quality control was always a bit up and down, but in their day they were better than, say, Dunlop, who produced wonderful compounds but not quite such good tyres!'

Bert Baldwin responds to Gardner's criticism that the front tyres were not developed. 'That's nonsense. I know Derek very well but myself, who was chief engineer, and the designer spent all night long in the Goodyear plant in Luxemburg doing high-speed testing – we did it all through the night because that was the only time we could get on the machine. We were there purely on the 10-inch tyres.'

Development on the rear tyres but not the fronts? 'No, that never was the Goodyear policy. It was always fairness and, as I say, I was the chief engineer and I was working on the tyre. We didn't stop any development on anything. Why do it if you're not going to work with it? Goodyear being such a big company, they wouldn't want that sort of reputation. I think quite frankly it was a poor concept, really.

'The project [the 10-inch tyre] was limited by the concept. The front tyre circumference is only 0·625 of the rear tyre, therefore it rotates at a much faster rate. For every rotation of the rear tyre the front tyre rotates 1·6 times. This means the front is travelling 1·6 times more than the rear, so when the rear is at 200mph the front is doing equivalent to 320mph. This causes the front tyre to distort.'

The 1977 team, here at Zolder (Phipps/Sutton). Gardner and Peterson talk technicalities at Silverstone where Tyrrell needs only two wheels to survey the six-wheeler (Phipps/Sutton).

There were tantalising glimpses of what might have been. Peterson set fastest lap in the US Grand Prix at Watkins Glen a full mile an hour faster than the next man, Hunt. Gardner confirms that in the speed trap the car was substantially quicker, as much as 8 to 10mph. 'Yes, that's right.'

Gardner 'liked Ronnie as a driver but, in terms of reporting back to us what was going on . . . he was hopeless. He got into the car, and he drove it. And that was it! Ronnie's natural way was to drive around a problem, rather than try to solve it.

'Ronnie always had colossal brake pad wear so I deduced he was using the throttle and the brakes at the same time – that was one of the reasons he was so quick, using this karting technique. I instrumented the car to prove it one way or the other, and in fact he never used the brake and throttle together at all. But still the brake pad wear was fantastic, so much higher than Patrick's – 50 per cent higher – and I never did find a reason, other than the fact that he was simply driving so much on the brakes. Jody's pad wear was slightly higher than Patrick's, too, because he tended to be rougher with a car: he'd take it by the scruff of the neck, whereas Patrick became part of it much more. Their driving techniques were completely different.'

The P34 made its final appearance at the Japanese Grand Prix in October, and the season finished with Depailler on 20 points and Peterson on 7. And Peterson was leaving. 'I seem to have a strange ability to change to a team when it's at the very top and then just ride down with it.'

Tyrrell would say: 'Looking at 1977 it is easy to condemn the six wheels but in 1976 the potential was there: recall the Swedish Grand Prix and the Scheckter-Depailler double. However, the imperatives of a busy calendar play against cars of complicated conception and favour those which are relatively simple. We learned that when a season is in full flow it is better to concentrate on sharpening the blade than making a better knife. Patrick threw himself body and soul into the six-wheel project. He took part from the beginning in all the development programme, and that was real work. Jody Scheckter left in the middle, Ronnie Peterson took his place, then he too left. But Patrick stayed, and that raised him in my estimation.'

Looking at things from a different angle: Depailler and Peterson at Long Beach, 1977 (Schlegelmilch).

Reflecting on the P34, Depailler would say: 'Yes, I believe and I will always believe, in spite of the setback which at the end finished the project. I remain convinced that the concept was valid. It was the realisation which failed, it was the methods which failed. And it's that which explains that after so much investment, as soon as I saw it wasn't going anywhere, I decided to do everything I could to make sure it was abandoned as quickly as possible. I know that this attitude could be badly understood, that certain people judged me fickle, but my reaction was the measure of my disappointment.

'I attached myself to this car as if it was my own child in spite of its faults, in spite of its caprices, because it was the expression of a great idea. End of '76, we did the assessment, we knew what it would take to correct the weaknesses in the first P34. I had already received offers from other front line teams. I pushed them away because I had the conviction that the new six-wheeler would be super-competitive. But in wanting to do everything himself, to resolve everything in his own way, Gardner lost his way. Instead of improving the six-wheeler, he only succeeded in exaggerating its faults. He made it heavier, made it even more difficult to drive and exploit. He led us into an impasse. It's why, at the end, I hold it against him. His talent was not in question. But, by his methods, he carries the responsibility for the failure.'

Gardner had never read this (Depailler's book has never been translated into English) and, since I was including it, natural justice demanded that he be given right of reply. This has become more poignant because the six-wheeler is still being raced, and successfully, in historic Formula 1 races. When I had read Depailler's words out to him he said: 'I see. What you have to see 25 years on is that the car can now be demonstrated with tyres which are compatible with each other and state of the art. Nothing else has changed on the car, nothing at all. The car is the same weight, the car has the same aerodynamics. And that car has proved itself to be ultra competitive so I don't really have to say anything about it other than the results.'

There is a sub-plot, which proceeded in the background of 1977. Gardner describes it and it centres around Renault, who – at Silverstone – had entered their own turbo-powered car, the first in Grand Prix racing. The sub-plot was that Tyrrell might run a six-wheeler with just this engine.

'Well, in 1977 we had a heck of a lot on our plates. I'd begun to despair of getting more horsepower from the Ford, even though the Cosworth people had put away their toys for a bit, and had started to concentrate on development. Anyway, the Renault engine was there, and it was destined for a Tyrrell. The first thing was to put it into the six-wheel car, without interfering with the fairly heavy workload we had on the race cars. Maurice Phillippe had just come back from California, and I hired him to do just that. We

resurrected a workshop in the timber yard, and that was where it was done. This was in the middle of summer in 1977 – round about the time the Renault F1 car made its début at Silverstone. I left in September, after Monza, so I can't give you any information about what happened after that. It just didn't happen.

'It was all very strongly tied in with Elf. They sponsored the whole thing. They sponsored the development of the Renault engine, in fact. The 1.5-litre turbocharged V6 had tremendous possibilities. A lot of people used to refer to the Bible, and say you were going against natural creation to do such things! But in a short while, people were getting a colossal amount of horsepower, weren't they? When I saw the power and torque figures on the original engine, they were just mouth-watering – I couldn't wait to get it in the car. I still say that if Renault hadn't had delusions of grandeur, and had just concentrated on the engine [rather than building their own car as well] it might have happened a whole lot quicker. Before I left, we'd got a mock-up engine – at least I think it was a mock-up engine, I can't really remember – and a car in an advanced state. He was always a quick worker, Maurice . . .'

This is another tantalising glimpse of what, in the hands of Peterson and Depailler, might have been, a glimpse of what might have returned Tyrrell to championships. The Renault turbo, mocked like the P 34, would recreate Grand Prix racing. And if Tyrrell had been the only one running it . . .

There is a postscript, covering two subjects – Depailler

and the P34 – and it belongs, properly, to Ken Tyrrell himself. 'You must remember that during his first two seasons with us Patrick was learning and, when he came to maturity, we embarked on the P34 programme. The six-wheelers were perhaps the most complicated cars ever seen in Grand Prix racing, and certainly demanded the tuning of a certain specific driving style.

'Later events have demonstrated that the six-wheel concept failed, which indisputably cost Patrick two good years of his career. We don't deserve, however, to be damned for having tried a technical experiment which was one of the most passionate in the history of Grands Prix.'

And that's the Englishman talking passionately, as well as the Frenchman talking it.

Charles Hewlett captures aspects of just how English Ken Tyrrell was. 'I remember his community interest. It so happened that at the Queen's Silver Jubilee in 1977 there was controversy about whether anything was going to be done for it in Ockham. He rang up and said: "What's all this about the Jubilee? Come over and see me." So off I went to the timber yard and he listened carefully. "Look," he said, "I've got property, I've got facilities, there's bits and pieces up here which might be useful. What do you want?" I said: "Well, it's all in its infancy but your help is enormously welcome." He opened his drawer, took out his cheque book and gave us £250. And that put the Jubilee in Ockham on its feet. To raise £25 was a lot in those days, never mind £250 . . .'

The last word on P34 itself goes to Neil Davis. 'There are hundreds of cars – we built enough! – that never won races, so you have to say it was successful.'

These days a six-wheeler is owned by Simon Bull, a car enthusiast and one of the world's leading watch experts. He is an original presenter of the BBC's *Antiques Roadshow*. It is driven by Martin Stretton who came into contact with Derek Gardner in the early 1990s.

'Derek provided tremendous help,' Stretton says, 'and became my race engineer,' but not yet with the six-wheeler. We raced the 005'[13] – with success. 'Derek had unfinished business: the P34. Simon loves a challenge, he's a bit of an eccentric and we aquired the six-wheeler. Simon got it from a gentleman in Germany who had bought it from Jarier (see next chapter) or it went through one other person before the German. It was running but needing a complete rebuild. And we got it.

Exit Depailler from the 1977 British Grand Prix – brakes/accident (Schlegelmilch).

'The first thing that became apparent was that the tyres were critical to the whole project. Cooper Avon, and particularly a couple of their top employees – one of them being ex-Goodyear from the days the car was in Formula 1 – put a good case to their parent company in America and they agreed to make the tyres specially for us.' These were 10-inches, of course, but 'of the same construction' as they were supplying to the historic championship. They made them, tested them and they worked bloody well. Out of the box, we were front row of the grid in the first race.'

That was Monza, and Gardner says: 'The fact was, or the facts are, that at Monza the car was set up exactly as it had been for Ronnie Peterson, and more or less straight from the time that the engine was fired up Martin was as quick or quicker than anyone else. In that sense I feel vindicated, yes I do.'

Stretton insists that 'the six-wheeler is the best pre-ground effect car I have ever driven and I've driven ten or 11 Cosworth-engined cars, ground effect and non-ground effect. Where it's superior to say an 005 is its front-end turn-in. You can turn it into the corner at high speed. First time out at the Paul Ricard circuit – bearing in mind I had done six not very good laps at Donington just shaking it down – at Signes Corner,[14] which is very quick, the car was sliding through at 145mph giving me confidence. There's a very quick chicane at Paul Ricard and the first few times through there it was almost "I hope the back wheels aren't going to hit anything" but very quickly you adjust mentally to it and you can place it just as accurately as any other car. Now we've got the tyres there's nothing else wrong with it.'

TAILPIECES: 'Scheckter losing a wheel and not knowing? I've lost a wheel so I know what it's like,' says Stretton. 'You get massive understeer, it's like you've had a puncture. I didn't actually know I'd lost a wheel until I got back to the pits but I did know something was wrong. It happened at Brands Hatch in the first season – a component failure.'

Eoin Young relates that Mario Acquati, who runs the motorsport bookshop at Monza, 'did a deal with Goodyear via Ken to buy all the remaining six-wheeler front tyres when the Formula 1 project was abandoned. Every fast Fiat 500 in Milan suddenly sprouted the widest tyres you've ever seen . . .

'The Tyrrell marque was being honoured at Sears Point [the track in California] and the movie *Grand Prix* was celebrating some sort of anniversary with a showing nearby. We all went to the pre-show chat and poster signing and then went across the road to eat. Ken, as the honoured guest, had to go to the movie but he joined us later and, when we asked, he said the movie was pretty much as he remembered but that Oppenheimer had made a great speech. We said did he mean Frankenheimer [as in John Frankenheimer, the celebrated director of *Grand Prix*] and he said yes, he probably did . . .'

We must hope that Frankenheimer was not present at the showing and that, if he was, Tyrrell didn't actually call him Oppenheimer.

Guffaw.

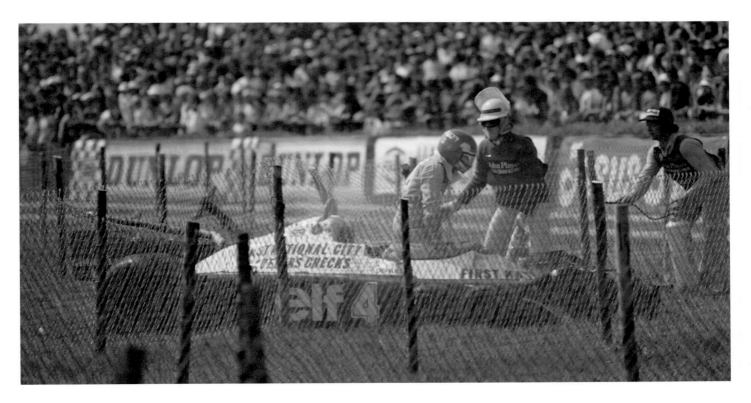

NOTES:

[1] Jenkinson, for long *Motor Sport* Grand Prix correspondent, was not averse to taking the mickey himself when he found suitable targets.

[2] 'In search of improved traction to handle the new-found power and sudden torque of the Cosworth DFV engine in 1968-69, Cosworth themselves, Lotus, Matra and McLaren all experimented with four-wheel-drive Formula 1 cars. After the final withdrawal of the 4WD Lotus 56B turbine car at the end of 1971, nothing came of these costly experiments' (*Autocourse History of the Grand Prix Car*, Nye).

[3] The transverse distance between a vehicle's wheels.

[4] Granatelli, legendary American motor racing figure who, in the late 1960s, designed, built and raced Indianapolis turbine cars.

[5] 007 was the Tyrrell which raced in 1974 to the beginning of 1976.

[6] Eoin Young, a New Zealand journalist who we've already met. He has exactly the sardonic sense of humour which would lead to a cuttings book making those with self-appointed importance seem foolish. Wish he had done it.

[7] *Depailler, La Course Est Un Combat* (José Rosinski, Calmann-Lévy, Paris, 1978).

[8] *Autosport*, 29 April 1976.

[9] *Autosport*, 10 June 1976.

[10] Of the Luxembourg test, more in a moment.

[11] Freddie Petersons, a Swedish journalist who was close to Peterson, does not recall him ever complaining about the six-wheeler.

[12] This remains a very sensitive area and I intend to respect Derek Gardner's wishes and leave it like that.

[13] 005 was the Tyrrell which raced at the end of 1972, in 1973 and the beginning of 1974.

[14] Signes, the right-hander at the end of the tremendously fast Mistral Straight.

Chapter Six

OVERTAKEN

"I got hepatitis in the June and I was very sick. He said to me: "You cannot do the British Grand Prix unless you beat me at tennis." I played tennis with him, I beat him – and I drove.

Jean-Pierre Jarier

'Right after the crash I walked back to the pits and one of the first people I saw was Ken. He was livid. I looked him in the eye and I said: "I'm sorry, it was my fault," and all he said was "again".'

Derek Daly

'I mean, he almost didn't think that the dinner was any good unless he'd had an argument. He loved that, and you'd better be sure of your position and you'd better be ready to defend it and you'd better be knowledgeable about it. He was just great with that stuff.'

Danny Sullivan

Keeping the story chronological, Depailler partnered Didier Pironi in 1978 (Depailler fifth in the Championship, Pironi 15th); Jean-Pierre Jarier partnered Pironi in 1979 (Jarier and Pironi joint tenth). Pironi, a handsome Parisian with a taste in exceptionally beautiful women, was ambitious – he fully intended to be France's first World Champion – and came from Formula 2, although he'd taken a risk by going one rung back down the ladder by competing in the Formula 3 support race to the Grand Prix at Monaco. He won it, and Ken Tyrrell noticed.

THE DRIVER'S STORY, PART 1 – Jean-Pierre Jarier, who'd been in Grand Prix racing since 1971.

'My speaking good English? As a Formula 2 driver I lived in Fulham, in Onslow Gardens. I'd done two races with Lotus

The joy of the first victory for four years: Michele Alboreto wins the 1982 Caesars Palace Grand Prix at Las Vegas (Phipps/Sutton).

in 1978 [USA East and Canada, which he led]. Then I went to Tyrrell and I started the season with Pironi. That first year I got a few podiums but we didn't have the turbo engine which nearly everybody else had. We had no sponsor and very little testing with the car – no money. The year after, Pironi went and I stayed. I had Derek Daly with me.

'No, I didn't know Ken. I was offered a drive by Paul Newman in Can-Am and I should have done that but I didn't because I wanted to go Formula 1 and I wanted a one-year contract which would leave me free to join a top team [in fact, as we shall see, he signed for two years]. I knew that Tyrrell didn't have the right engine, I knew he didn't have a sponsor. It was really difficult but I signed anyway. It was a mistake as far as my career was concerned but Ken was a personality, a nice person to work with and the car was reliable. He had good mechanics. Maurice Phillippe was a bit too old, but it was a good team.

Depailler and his new team-mate Didier Pironi, rich, handsome and with a penchant for beautiful women (Phipps/Sutton).

'The first season was not bad considering that the other teams had better engines. We were always there even with no money, no money, no money because we had no sponsor. Suddenly the second year he got the money from Candy. Yes, I had the impression that the team was moving downhill because, you know, it was at its best and the best at the beginning of the 1970s – the first team to really go testing in Kyalami, the only team to go testing for three weeks.

'They had Stewart. They had the Matra monocoque, which was the best. Matra was a fighter plane company so they had a very nice chassis, Stewart was World Champion with it and the team was organised very well, but after Stewart left it was not such a good team. McLaren, Lotus, Williams, they had young people, young engineers. Ken was very, very good but he couldn't fit with the new period, a new way of motor racing. The new way means a lot of money and a lot of people in the team, it means you pay for a very good engineer.

'I stayed the second year because I had a two-year contract and then it was too late. The second year we were still stuck with the Ford engine and Maurice was very old. Ken was a nice guy: I got hepatitis in the June and I was

very sick. He said to me: "You cannot do the British Grand Prix unless you beat me at tennis to prove you are fit!" I played tennis with him, I beat him and I drove.

'The atmosphere was really good. At Paul Ricard you had lunch with him at the hotel, rose wine, and it was very nice. He enjoyed all that, he really did. It was like a family – but Pironi would look at that and conclude he had no chance to be World Champion. We all knew that, we all could see that, so in a sense it was the older way of working.

'An example. We come to the Brazilian Grand Prix – a couple of years before [in 1975] with the Shadow.[1] Ken knew I was able to take the corner after the pits flat out, fifth gear but I couldn't do it with this car.'

Dialogue . . .

Jarier: 'The steering wheel is beginning to be very heavy in the corner. The chassis is bending. I cannot turn the wheel because all the front of the car is bending.'

Tyrrell (disbelieving and having the car put up on jacks): 'The steering is very light.'

Depailler: 'Yes, but you are not in the corner, you are on the jacks! You don't have the stress on the car.'

Tyrrell: 'It's impossible the chassis is bending.'

At this point Maurice Phillippe 'went under the car and discovered that the monocoque was completely cracked – because the team had no money,' Jarier says. 'It cracked because of too much stress and they did not have carbon, they had nothing. We were racing like five years before. If he had had more money he would have got a top engineer, gone testing and had very good conditions. He was nearly on the point of cheating with the weight of the car and a few other details because he wanted to win races so badly – but he couldn't, he couldn't do it. He didn't work in the same way as Frank Williams and Ron Dennis, he couldn't see the future like them. It is necessary to be a very hard person – no sentiment . . .

'I got on very, very well with Pironi. I was a bit older than him and he had respect for me. I knew him when he was 12 in the Paris suburbs so I didn't have any trouble at all, and with Ken it was OK. Pironi went to Ferrari [via Ligier] because we were not able to win Grands Prix with

the car. Under the huge pressure of the public and the press there he changed completely and had a big fight with Gilles Villeneuve. With me he didn't do that.'

TAILPIECE: 'I bought a P34 six-wheeler, the one which was driven by Ronnie Peterson, and that was a result of the family atmosphere,' says Jarier.

Dialogue . . .

Tyrrell: 'Jean-Pierre, we are running out of money a bit. If you are interested in this car it's £20,000.'

Jarier: 'OK, I buy it.'

Conclusion: 'I made £50,000 on it, but the money being made today, it looks like nothing.' (Keeping it in the family, we will be meeting this car again.)

In 1980, Jarier finished joint tenth with Daly in the World Championship (as did Rosberg, Villeneuve and John Watson!) while a young New Zealander, Mike Thackwell, made a bizarre début in the Canadian Grand Prix.

THE DRIVER'S STORY, PART 2 – Derek Daly, who'd been in Grand Prix racing since 1978 and driven three times for Tyrrell in 1979: Austria then the last two races, Canada and USA East.

'Austria? Oh that's right, the left front brake disc broke and I went through the cornfield. I literally saw the car mow the corn down ahead of me. Jarier had hepatitis so Tyrrell needed a fill-in driver for two or three races. How I got to drive in Austria was that he put Geoff Lees in for Germany and I had just won two Formula 2 races in Italy. I called Ken up myself and asked if he would give me a trial run in Austria, which he agreed to do. And it went very well. No, no, I did not have to pay him. Never paid him. He was impressed enough to give me Canada and the USA. What I enjoyed about it was he almost personally took me into the team and personally looked after me. I don't know why. I was his project. I think he did that a lot with drivers.

'I got more directions, believe it or not, after the races. I can distinctly remember the South African Grand Prix at

the start of '80. I had trouble with the gearshift and took the corners off the dogs[2] and I couldn't get fourth gear. Afterwards he sent me the dog ring in the post and said: "I want you to see what happened, I want you to get down here so I can demonstrate to you what these gears do so you can visualise it and know how to change gear to save these in future." Like a schoolmaster! I went down, he showed me and I never had any more trouble.

'In 1980, the multiple crash at the start of Monaco was one of the most famous pieces of video ever used. And during practise I hit the front suspension and broke something on that – and I'd hit a few things. Right after the crash I walked back to the pits and one of the first people I saw was Ken. He was livid. I looked him in the eye.'

Dialogue . . .

Daly: 'I'm sorry, it was my fault.'

Tyrrell: 'Again.'

And, Daly says, 'That was it. He never said another word to me for the rest of the weekend. Monaco was just such an important event to him.

'He could be volatile at times. I remember at the Dutch Grand Prix it was myself and Jarier. The cars were very well balanced, we ran out of things to change and in terms of time we were quite close to each other. We were off the pace but we had no real problems with the car. We were going as fast as the cars went but the fact that we were off the pace meant a logical discussion suddenly turned into almost a rage: IF THERE'S NOTHING WRONG WITH THE CARS, HOW COME YOU DIDN'T GO QUICKER?! He was not accepting that it was the cars which could not go faster.

'In Holland a disc broke – that was a huge crash. I was braking for Tarzan[3] and the left front brake disc just exploded. I was braking down from 190mph. It tore the front suspension off and I just ploughed straight on – luckily there was a tyre barrier. The car somersaulted and landed outside the track. I got to see the sky, and that was actually the second time I had collapsed when they took me out of a racing car. That scared me so much. I had a vision of all the serious injuries that I had never had in a racing car. I knew they were coming that day and when they took

me out I just felt dizzy and collapsed. In fact I was fine, four stitches on my left shin, that was all. He called me up next day and said: "All I want to say is I apologise that you had a crash of that magnitude in one of my cars."

'Montreal? Nelson Piquet and Alan Jones started banging off each other going through the fast esses. They hit each other, caused a big pile up and of course we were the cars following on. I ran into somebody. Jarier was in the same crash and there was only one car left, which was Mike Thackwell's. They took it and put Jarier into it.' This gave Thackwell what is believed to be, or was then, the shortest Grand Prix début ever. It could be measured in yards.

'The leaving? Quite honestly I don't know whether Eddie Cheever brought any money but I had had such a bad year with so many crashes – a lot of them not my fault – and I believe Candy [the sponsors] might have had a preference for Cheever, being Italian-born and speaking fluent Italian. It was just like a normal part of it: didn't work, move on. Ken told me straight, absolutely. It did not affect his feelings towards me as a person.'

Pironi (no 3) at the 1978 Monaco Grand Prix where he'd finish fifth. Depailler (no 4) won (all Phipps/Sutton).

TAILPIECE: 'Believe it or not, when I left Formula 1 in 1982 it was I think 11 years before I went to a race again. In the meantime I started doing broadcasting for IndyCar racing in the States, which was broadcast in Britain. When I went back one of the first people I met was Ken and immediately he sat me down and started telling me all about the things that I was doing. His biggest complaint was that Norah said I didn't sound the same anymore. I don't like to say I have the American accent but you do have to bend some of the words because otherwise they don't understand it. All the time they ask: "What was that?" and you have to rephrase it. Anyway, it was exactly Ken Tyrrell being British . . . '

So, at the end of 1980, Daly went and Cheever came. He finished 1981 joint 11th. An Argentine, Ricardo Zunino, did the first two races (and was 13th in both) before Michele Alboreto joined. He'd stay three years and represent real hope of recovery although in 1981 he couldn't win a point. Cheever went and was replaced by a Swede, Slim Borgudd. In 1982, he did the first three races for Tyrrell (and was nowhere near scoring a point).

THE DRIVER'S STORY, PART 3 – Brian Henton, who'd been in Grand Prix racing since 1975.

'Borgudd did up to USA West and he ran out of money, I think. At the time Ken was short of finance and a friend of mine was very friendly with him. He suggested Ken put me in. I was under no illusions that if anyone came with any large sponsorship I would have to stand down. I took it because I didn't have a drive. I didn't think I was near the end of my career. You don't – until nobody hires you.

'I had won every championship I had ever competed in, but I'd never got to grips with Formula 1 because I hadn't had the machinery that could do it. I was always in cars rather like Ken's: under-developed or under-financed and, on some occasions, both.

The Monaco win always seems sweetest of all to generation after generation. Depailler in full delight (Phipps/Sutton).

'Ken was a very careful and pragmatic person, one of the most honest guys in Formula 1. Whereas most teams in Ken's position would have used this year's sponsorship to pay last year's bills, Ken was always very straight both with his personnel and with his sponsors. It's well documented how some of those names which are now very near the front of the grid survived, what with sitting in Saudi palaces for six weeks til you got your cheque . . .

'Ken always kept within his budget and motor racing is rather like football: the manager only needs two more players and he's got a winning team. In motor racing, you listen to the drivers and designers – and they'll say a certain spending on a modification here and a modification there and you've got it, although of course it very rarely works out like that. Ken would only spend within his budget. It's a very old-fashioned and traditional approach.

'The Tyrrell team were in premises that were wonderfully adequate in the earlier days but now it was getting to the era when if you didn't have your own wind tunnel, and composite factory and all ultra-modern equipment you just weren't going to be up there, no matter how innovative you were. The woodyard had a wonderful atmosphere and it's quite interesting that you could almost map the changing face of Formula 1 there as Ken came to his twilight years.

'Alboreto was a fantastic bloke. Ken only actually employed drivers that he either respected or liked. You got the impression that even if someone came along with a massive budget and Ken hadn't got money, if he didn't think the driver would fit in he probably wouldn't have employed him.'

(Tyrrell once said: 'The most important contribution a manager can make is to build a team of people who can and will work together. You can have a group of eight very good mechanics but if just one of them doesn't fit in with the others you get aggravation.')

'I did the fastest lap in the British Grand Prix [at Brands Hatch],' Henton says. 'It just shows how small a gap it is from the back of the grid to the front, in actual fact – especially when you get in to race trim when nobody has special tyres and engines or whatever, and you find yourself on a more level playing field. Even with the total lack of finance and some of the development facilities, the Tyrrell car was still a good car. Some of those people had been there years and years and years and they knew how to build a bloody good Formula 1 car.

'That lap was quick and in a DFV-engined car against Lauda and all these others, and against Renault turbos and Ferrari turbos. If you look at the driver quality in the 1982 season, there was probably more people who'd won Grands Prix and ex-World Champions capable of doing the business than ever before or since. It was a very competitive year.

'The lap itself? At the time you don't even think about it because, believe it or not, you know that the car is responding to what you are doing and, if you are comfortable with the thing, you can take it nearer to its limit than you can if it's misbehaving. The car that I drove wasn't my own, it was Alboreto's spare and it worked very, very well on that day. There's a lot of very tricky cambered bends at Brands and there were places where in terms of straight line speed you didn't stand a chance, but in terms of grip versus weight it worked. Maurice Phillippe[4]

designed that one and it had the shock absorbers and all the springs were in board so it had very little unsprung weight on the wheels.'

Although Henton didn't get a point, Alboreto finished joint seventh in the championship with 25 and, at Las Vegas in the United States Grand Prix he gave the Tyrrell team their first victory since Monaco in 1978. This was overshadowed by the fact that Rosberg won the World Championship from Watson. Alboreto, in Nigel Roebuck's phrase, 'drove a brilliant race, pacing himself, his car and tyres to perfection.' He'd qualified on the second row and spent long laps tracking Alain Prost (Renault) – but Prost's tyres were making the car vibrate violently and, on lap 52, Alboreto outbraked him. He beat Watson by 27.292 seconds.

Henton was leaving. 'In those days almost all the drivers were on a yearly contract and it was a battle at the end of the season about who went where. It was almost like snakes and ladders – A went to B so you possibly went to C. You didn't even have to be told you weren't being retained. That was just the facts of life. I was watching who went where and trying to get a spot. I hired the car myself in that Race of Champions [5] to try and put myself in the shop window.'

It didn't work.

TAILPIECE: 'Of all the people I know in motor racing, Ken was one of the few that I socialised with because we both enjoyed country pursuits. Even right up to his death he used to come up to Ingasby, where I've an estate in Leicestershire, and shoot with us. I used to also shoot with him at Chatsworth with Paul Tear[6]. I'd see him at the British Grand Prix once a year. I only went to one, that one, because I'm a member of the BRDC. We'd catch up on who was doing what and talk about the old days. He was enthusiastic and knowledgeable right to the end.'

So Henton went, Alboreto stayed and an American came.

THE DRIVER'S STORY, PART 4 – Danny Sullivan.
'The guy who got me into racing and who got me

hooked up with Tyrrell is Dr Frank Falkner. Frank was a long-time buddy of Ken's and John Cooper before they ever even made the Cooper Formula Junior car, but Frank's a doctor, so it was a hobby. I met Ken and Jackie Stewart and Norah at the US Grand Prix [in 1970]. I was coming over to do the Jim Russell School and Ken said: "Well, come a little bit early and stay a weekend with us." That was the weekend of non-championship race [the International Trophy] at Silverstone. I came over and did the school just before Monaco and when that was over Ken said: "Come on down and stay with us. We hear you've got some talent." So I went down and worked as a gofer for him and then I worked down the road. I stayed about two months but it wasn't very fair to them. Norah was having back problems.

'I admired the hell out of Ken. He was tough, he was stern, he was kind but he was really firm. I would imagine he was a pretty tough father, but fair. One of the things about Ken was that he loved a good argument. I don't mean a fight, I mean a debate. And when it was over it was over. He almost didn't think that the dinner was any good unless he'd had an argument. He loved that, and you better be sure of your position and you'd better be ready to defend it and you'd better be knowledgable about it. He was just great with that stuff.

'I had some help to do Formula Ford in 1972 when I came back, then I went and did my own thing, but I remained friends with them. I wasn't going off to the Grands Prix or anything. I was trying to get a career. It must have been 1973 or '74 that I bought a Transit van off him, one of those 35cwt Fords to pull a trailer for Formula 3. He sold it to me for twenty quid. The deal was I had to sell it back to him – for twenty quid! It was a way of helping me out, and it was a transaction. It was also a great help.

'In 1978 I ran out of steam, went back to the States and did CanAm etc etc. I had pretty good success. Frank called Ken again in the winter of 1982, around November, beginning of December. Ken was having a test for a seat because he had money from Benetton,[7] it was at Paul Ricard and the young stars like Stefan Johansson and

Beppe Gabbiani would be there. Frank secured me an invitation.

'I'll never forget it. I arrived with a guy that was backing me in CanAm, Garvin Brown, who was an heir to Jack Daniels. I was in my driving suit.'

Dialogue . . .

Tyrrell: 'Before you drive you've got to sign this contract.'

Sullivan read it and was taking his suit off when Brown walked in.

Brown: 'What are you doing? What's the matter?'

Sullivan: 'I can't drive the car.'

Brown: 'What do you mean?'

Sullivan: 'Have you seen this contract? It says if I'm quickest and I get chosen for the drive I have to cover my own expenses and the amount he's offering won't do that. I can't afford to drive for Ken!'

Sullivan was at least making a living in the States. He remembers the contract was for £10,000, but of course he didn't live in Europe and didn't have a house in Europe so he'd have to travel long distance. He wasn't reckoning on doing this first class, 'I'm talking about just doing it.' Moreover, of the 16 races one was in South Africa, another in Brazil – not exactly cheap places to fly to. Sullivan thought Brown ought to have taken the whole thing as an insult.

Brown: 'If you get the drive, I'll pay your salary.'

Sullivan: 'OK.'

He got dressed again. 'I'd been watching all the guys fitting the seats and changing the pedals and changing the steering wheel and everything. I'm the last guy and it's almost dark. It's winter time, so it's getting dark at 5 o'clock. I'm sitting there in the car thinking this and thinking that. Roger Hill – I knew all these guys from when I was a gofer – leant into the car and said: "A word of advice." I said: "Yes?" He said: "Just drive the car." I was trying to be professional like everybody else, dammit! So I just put the seat belts on and went out and did it. Every lap I was quicker and quicker and from the second lap, faster

Jean-Pierre Jarier came in to join Pironi in 1979 and finished third in the British Grand Prix. Here he is – on the way, and celebrating. Clay Regazzoni and René Arnoux looked pleased too (Phipps/Sutton).

than anybody else. My increments weren't half a second at a time, I wasn't that impressive. It was like two tenths, then another tenth, then another tenth – that type of thing.' What followed, Sullivan insists, was typical of Tyrrell and his economy of language.

Dialogue . . .

Tyrrell: 'Can you be in Brazil on such and such a date?'

Sullivan: 'Yeah.'

Tyrrell: 'OK, well be there then.'

And that, Sullivan adds, was it. 'He didn't say: "You've got the job" or anything like that. He didn't waste words.'

Got the drive? Not at all. Sullivan had been invited to the annual tyre test at the Jacarepagua circuit. Waste words? 'Ken was the most difficult guy to have a conversation with on the phone. All my conversations with Ken were very short, not because he was rude or anything, it was just that he didn't waste words and he didn't get into long conversations about anything, particularly on the phone.

'So we go to Brazil. I wanted to do the right thing, and Garvin and I went down two or three days early to get acclimatised. And then I sat. I sat every day all day and never got in the car. Never, OK, until the last half of the last day. Ken puts me in the car and I go out on a set of control[8] tyres. He gave me a minimal amount of laps, say ten, for learning the circuit. I'd been all over the circuit watching everybody practice but you still haven't put it together in a car. He then sticks on a set of used qualifiers – Michele had used them – and, if you remember, Rio was a really long track. I went out and I was only three or four tenths off the time when they were brand new.

'That was it. At the end of the test I was "well???" because he still hadn't said anything. Then he said: "You selected yourself" and off he goes to the airport! During the week we'd had dinner, he and Garvin and I, but you don't ask because you don't want to jeopardise it – like if we're pushing too hard.

Clockwise from top left: Animated conversation with team member Brian Lisles at Hockenheim (Phipps/Sutton). Jarier stayed for 1980, to be joined by Derek Daly and, briefly, Mike Thackwell. This is Jarier at Monaco, qualifying. He was involved in a crash at the start of the race (Phipps/Sutton). Tyrrell ran three cars at the 1980 Canadian Grand Prix (Phipps/Sutton). Derek Daly at Monaco in 1980 (Phipps/Sutton).

'They had the non-championship race at Brands in '83 [see Note 5] and I did that and had a real good result. Michele didn't do it. I had that dice with Keke right there at the end and I finished just a nose behind.

'Ken got really upset with me at one of the races. He said: "You're too nice." Other teams had the turbo cars and they'd be coming up to lap me. He said: "Don't you let those guys by." I said: "But Ken, the guy was lapping me." He said "I don't care. They've got to find a way by. That's their job. It's not your job to help them." That was him teaching you about being a Grand Prix driver and what it needed.

'One of the reasons young drivers turned out to be a talent was that Ken taught you a lot – not how to drive the car, he wasn't a driver coach telling you that you were at the wrong place at the apex. You had that talent when you came there. Ken educated you in how to be a race car driver and a good one, how to handle things and fight for things. That enables the talent to flower and that is where he was really, really brilliant. I thought a lot of Ken and I think everybody else did – that's one of the reasons why all of the other teams were always looking at Ken's drivers to cherry pick them!

'Norah was a general's wife. The general is the guy who commands the troops and leads the charge. He has a job to do and it is a very consuming job but she was always there for what he needed: not in the way, not if he had big business meetings, but if he was going to dinner she was the perfect companion – the perfect wife in that she knew what he needed to do and she knew how to supplement that. She was a partner as well as a wife, and she had her own characteristics and her own talent.'

The season had begun in Brazil (Sullivan 11th, Alboreto did not finish) and moved to Long Beach for the USA West (Sullivan eighth, Alboreto ninth) before the Race of Champions. In France, Alboreto was eighth, Sullivan did not finish; at Imola neither finished; and that brought them to Monaco where Sullivan qualified on the last row of the grid. Light rain was falling at the start of the race.

Dialogue . . .

Tyrrell: 'Do you want to start on slicks or wets?'

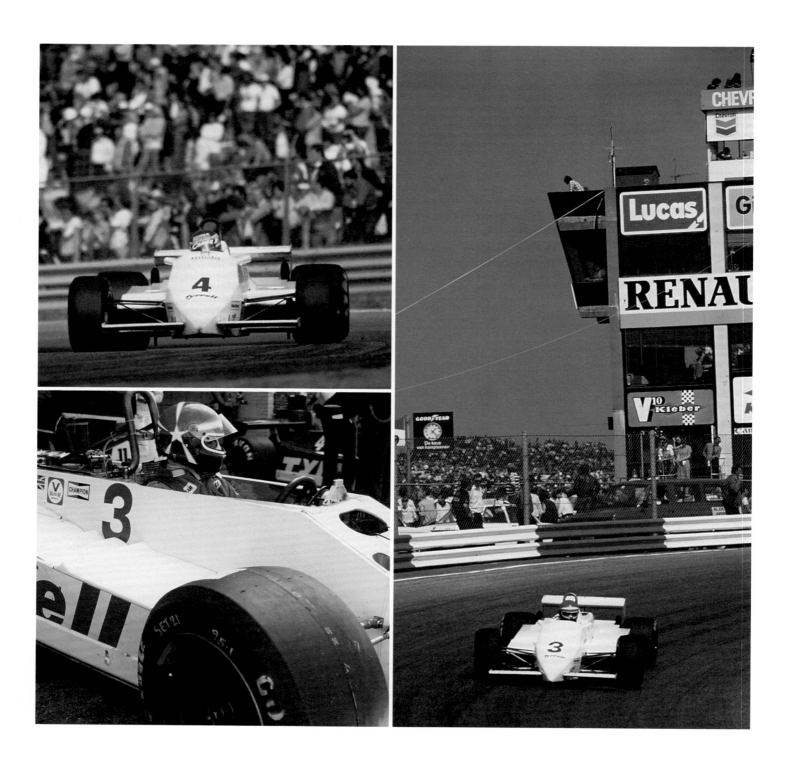

Sullivan (rolling his eyes and looking at the sky): 'Are you crazy? Of course wets.'

Tyrrell: 'I thought you were going to start on slicks.'

Sullivan: 'Ken, it's raining.'

Tyrrell: 'It's going to stop.'

As Sullivan points out, 'in those days we didn't make the pit stops and if you did, you really hurt yourself in terms of time lost. I'm sitting on the grid next to Elio de Angelis in the JPS Lotus and Elio's looking at me like "are you crazy?" I'm sitting there with my hands in the air saying: "It's nothing to do with me."

'The race started, somebody touched the barrier here, somebody there, somebody at Loews Hairpin, somebody at the Swimming Pool and I am going . . . so . . . slowly. I'm going round thinking: "What a wanker!" I . . . was . . . creeping. I had no grip, no nothing. At the end of the first lap I thought it again. "My God, what a wanker you really are." Then with all those cars going off I thought, "Well, maybe not that big a wanker . . ."'

On that opening lap Alboreto and Nigel Mansell (Lotus) crashed and Sullivan began to move up, so that by lap 9 he was 11th.

'The thing is, 23 laps into the race or something like that, Ken was 100 per cent right. It was drying out. Then it got completely dry and people had to make pit stops and I was lucky, I passed a couple of cars. The Tyrrell was a normally aspirated car: it wasn't as good as the Williams and it wasn't as good as the McLaren but it was good – not a great car, not phenomenal, but really good. I had no complaints about the thing.'

Carefully, Sullivan took the Tyrrell to fifth at the end, albeit a lap down.

Sullivan was 12th at Spa and Alboreto 14th; and they went to Detroit where Alboreto qualified on the third row and Sullivan the eighth. Sullivan retired with an electrical problem but Alboreto prepared to exploit the nimbleness of his car and the nip-and-dart nature of the street circuit. He chased Nelson Piquet (Brabham) and when Piquet slowed near the end for a puncture he sailed by. He finished 7.702 seconds ahead of Rosberg (Williams), and that was the last Tyrrell win.

It was also, of course, the last time a ritual was enacted at the factory far away at Ockham and one of the men who did it, Keith Boshier, explains that.

'A couple of the lads would ring up, I used to load my ladder on to the roofrack and go to the factory, get on the roof and put the Union Jack up. Just how early we started doing this I don't know. Most of the wins were up to 1973 and the races weren't on television in those days, but you could get them on French radio. I can't speak French very well but you'd get the gist of who was leading and so on. I'm not sure we ever had to get up in the middle of the night although I've a feeling we went out one evening in the dark and did it. The flag would stay up for a couple of days.

'I remember once we had a problem because we put the flag up and a member of the royal family had died. We wondered what we should do and Derek Gardner came out. "What are you on about?" We told him it was a bit awkward. He said: "Oh dear, oh dear, I think we've got to get our priorities right over these things." That was it – the flag stayed up.'

Anyway, on the evening of 5 June 1983 the Union Jack was hoisted and would be hoisted no more.

By autumn, approaching the European Grand Prix at Brands Hatch, Alboreto had 10 points and Sullivan the two from Monaco. Sullivan qualified on the tenth row and Alboreto last of all. Sullivan remembers that.

'I outqualified Michele by a second – my car was working good and Michele's wasn't.' Sullivan arrived on the Sunday morning and as he got out of his car Alboreto was waiting for him.

Dialogue . . .

Alboreto: 'I didn't have anything to do with it.'

Sullivan: 'What the hell are you talking about?'

Alboreto: 'I didn't have anything to do with it.'

Alboreto walked away and Tyrrell walked over.

Tyrrell: 'We are taking your car and giving it to Michele.'

Sullivan (going 'ballistic'): 'What do you mean, you're giving my car? You can't take my car!'

In 1981 Eddie Cheever and Michele Alboreto were the principal drivers. This is Alboreto (no 4) at the French Grand Prix . . . and Cheever (all Phipps/Sutton).

Looking back now, Sullivan points out that 'Michele wasn't in the hunt for the championship, there wasn't anything at stake. I got in a big heated argument with Ken and I didn't win. I got the other car and I got the guys to change the car exactly. I remember I had an argument with the chief engineer about that. He had calculated changing the rollbar – because Michele had a softer rollbar – but I wanted the car exactly like mine. When they'd done that the car was just like the one they'd given to Michele and just as quick.'

Neither finished, Alboreto out with an engine problem, Sullivan with a fire.

'After the race Ken said: "I'd have been really disappointed with you if you hadn't argued that hard for your car. I wouldn't have given it to you, but I wouldn't have thought you'd have the fire to ever make it as a driver." That was Ken, that was his personality, that was his character trait.'

Caesars Palace, 1982. Alboreto started from the second row and beat John Watson (McLaren) by 27 seconds (Phipps/Sutton).

Sullivan was leaving. 'Ken told me instantly and I knew that there was maybe a chance he'd lose Benetton. He said they wanted a turbo charged car and could I wait until February? I called Doug Shierson [who'd bought a Lola for the IndyCar series and wanted to run Sullivan]. I asked him: "How long can you give me?" and it was like a week. The two times didn't come even close to each other.

'Ken said to me later, when it was all done, he was disappointed that I chose not to continue, but I was put in a position by him. I went back to the States after the last race and I went to an IndyCar race, just for practice one afternoon. I saw Doug Shierson, he liked European racing and he'd followed it quite closely. He offered me a job while Ken said: "I'm losing Benetton and I don't know if I can honour our contract." He had all the options, obviously, to terminate or not but he was warning me of the situation. He was not dishonest, quite the opposite. He was 110 per cent straight.

'Frank Falkner sat in his house in California for three days, phone calls back and forth. Frank would call Ken and talk to him, and I'd ask him a question. They'd put down the phone and we'd debate more. Ken said he might have to take a pay driver, somebody who could bring some money to the table, and I wasn't that guy. Ultimately, I called and said I really, really didn't want to go to IndyCar racing I wanted to stay in Formula 1 but . . . '

TAILPIECE: 'I have driven for quite a few teams over the years. Ken Tyrrell didn't have the money but it was the best-run team that I had ever been with. Penske was close. I'm talking about efficiency: "Here's where you've got to be," no nonsense. Ken took care of everything. All you did was show up and do your job. If there was a hassle or something was going wrong you weren't brought into it. It wasn't like, "Oh, this is a problem" or "that's a problem" – other than, say, the car's handling wasn't right. Anything that didn't relate directly to you, you didn't know about, it was just done. Your job was to drive the race car. Period.'

NOTES:
[1] Shadow was a Formula 1 team between 1973 and 1980, winning Austria in 1977.
[2] Dog rings, part of the gearbox.
[3] Tarzan was the horseshoe at the end of the pit lane straight, and a spectacular place to watch Grand Prix cars.
[4] Maurice Phillippe, who died in 1989, had worked for Colin Chapman at Lotus and joined Tyrrell in 1978. A quiet man, he was chief designer for ten years.
[5] The Race of Champions, a non-championship event, was at Brands Hatch on 10 April 1983. Thirteen drivers contested it and Keke Rosberg won from Danny Sullivan, Henton fourth.
[6] Paul Tear became a friend and I am indebted to him for allowing me to use extracts from his address at Tyrrell's memorial service. They appear in the final chapter.
[7] Benetton were Tyrrell's main sponsors in 1983.
[8] Control tyres are used in testing. They are a tyre with a known performance at that particular circuit and thus a good point of reference to work around, not least for the tyre manufacturers who may be experimenting with different compounds.

Chapter Seven

FAST MEN PASSING THROUGH

'Being close to Norah like that and loving her – from the outside it was very easy to feel it.'

Jean Alesi

'Ken told me he wasn't taking up the option. He sort of said "well, that's it." It was matter of fact: that's business, you know. He was trying to survive in a very harsh environment without any sponsors, really, so he had to do whatever he had to do to keep the thing going.'

Julian Bailey

'I remember him asking [other teams]: "Why are you worried?" and the reply was: "It doesn't work like that, Ken." I can't remember who said it. Dad wouldn't have done that, no, he would not have been a party to anything like that.'

Bob Tyrrell

Ken Tyrrell was very sure that Stefan Bellof would have been Germany's first world champion. In 1983, the two outstanding talents of Formula 3 – Ayrton Senna and Martin Brundle – were given a test day at McLaren, an enormously significant thing for a young man. Bellof was there that day, too, and there on merit.

In November Brundle tested for Tyrrell at Silverstone and was so fast he 'staggered' Tyrrell but, as Tyrrell pointed out, the team had no sponsorship and Brundle was unlikely to attract any because British companies didn't sponsor Grand Prix racing.

Stefan Bellof bestriding the storm at Monaco in 1984 – and catching Ayrton Senna before the race was stopped (Schlegelmilch).

That Christmas of 1983, or rather January of 1984 (when Tyrrell held their Christmas parties) Alboreto came over with his new wife Nadia. Alboreto, now with Ferrari, presented each member of the Tyrrell team with a plaque thanking them for what they had done for him, then posed with Tyrrell, who was clearly instructing him how to cut a three-tier cake . . .

Brundle went to the traditional Rio tyre test and, in late February, Tyrrell signed him. At this point Tyrrell toyed with signing Jonathan Palmer as well. Tyrrell was almost desperate: he had Sullivan on standby for the first Grand Prix at Rio in late March. A week later he signed Bellof, who had been given a brief test at Paul Ricard and gone faster than Brundle.

The race drowned, but Bellof (top) finished third – which was subsequently taken off him in Tyrrell's fuel controversy (Phipps/Sutton). Brundle at Monaco . . . he crashed in qualifying and didn't race (both Phipps/Sutton).

'We took Martin on and we should never have taken Martin on,' Bob Tyrrell says. 'I thought to a certain extent if we'd got a young British driver we'd attract sponsorship. When Martin came along with his dad, Ken said to him: "I don't want any sponsorship. We'll pay you." They were flabberghasted by that. They thought: it's Christmas! In hindsight there were very few British companies that sold consumer products all over the world under brand names.'

Only two teams, Tyrrell and Arrows, did not have turbo engines so each race except the street circuits was a test of prudence and persistence. The nimble Tyrrell with its quick-response Cosworth might do well round the streets, though . . .

Brundle slogged a fifth in Brazil and Bellof a sixth at Zolder, a fifth at San Marino. Monaco was wet (Brundle had crashed heavily in qualifying and did not start). Senna's drive in the Toleman has wreathed itself into folklore as, in the Toleman-Hart, he caught Prost and, if the race had not been stopped by the weather, would have beaten him easily. Because Tyrrell were subsequently expunged from the records for a fuel infringement – of that, more in a moment – Bellof's drive has been largely unexplored.

Let's explore it. He qualified last on the grid with a time of 1m 26.117s against Prost's pole of 1m 22.661s. Between them were 18 cars and this at Monaco where most overtaking moves are blocked or end in a coating of wreckage across the track.

Lap 1: Bellof 12th!

The rain teemed, cars dropped out here and there and, from laps 2 to 6, Bellof ran 11th before overtaking Jacques Laffite (Williams). On lap 9 Alboreto spun and stalled his Ferrari – eighth, and Bellof ran there until almost simultaneously Nigel Mansell (Lotus) crashed while he was leading and Bellof got past Manfred Winkelhock (ATS). Bellof had been pressing so hard that Winkelhock waved him through – sixth. Bellof went after Rosberg (Williams) got him at the chicane on lap 21 – fifth. Niki Lauda (McLaren) spun off – fourth and coming like a storm at René Arnoux's Ferrari. Bellof caught and hounded it through Casino Square and went – classically – to the inside for Mirabeau. Arnoux came across so hard that Bellof was briefly forced on to the pavement – third. This was lap 27, Prost leading Senna by seven seconds (no gap Senna-Bellof survives, I think). What has survived is that in the remaining four laps before the race was stopped Senna was within striking distance of Prost and each of those laps Bellof was catching Senna.

Tyrrell bellowed 'WHY?' when he saw the race being stopped and pointed out in a great outpouring of sound that the weather had been worse at the start.

Canada was for turbos but Detroit was another street circuit and here Brundle drove a beautifully mature race to finish second to Nelson Piquet (Brabham). Bellof had hoisted himself as high as sixth before he crashed.

Before the British Grand Prix, FISA banned the Tyrrell team from the rest of the season for what can be described as an alleged fuel irregularity. It was fiendishly complicated (do you know what Toluene and Zylene are?) and so I put it at its simplest: after Detroit, samples were taken from the fuel tank and from a tank for the car's water injection system. Supposedly, illegal additives were found in the former and lead bulbs, clearly for ballast, in the latter. If the car started with them that was fine, but if they were added during re-fuelling that wasn't.

FISA's procedures – confronting Tyrrell with evidence he had not seen and so forth – violated even the most basic

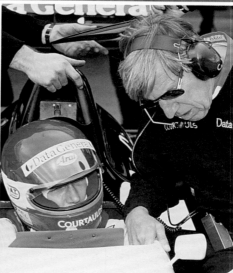

norms of justice. Using the courts Tyrrell was able to keep his team in the Grands Prix up to Holland, although their doings for the whole season were swept from all official records.

Ken Tyrrell was, his son Bob insists, 'a hard businessman but if things came up in Formula 1 like the bloody silly fuel tank in the normally aspirated days he'd say "what are they worried about? The turbos are one and a half seconds quicker than the normally aspirated car so why bother? We're not going to be winning the races so why? This is stupid, this is going over the top."

'His mentality was different. You have to have a business approach to Formula 1 because it is your business, but he didn't have a business approach to the sports side of it. Sometimes you'd have a guy who, for whatever reason, didn't qualify and so wasn't allowed to take part in the race. Other teams would say: "Well, we could be leading and if he's in he might interfere with our drivers, he could be a back marker who's going to slow us down." Dad wouldn't think about that because it wasn't sporting – although he was as hard as nails on other things.

'With the fuel tank thing, you had a situation where every other team was together on this because they all had turbos – including Ferrari. I remember him asking: "Why are you worried?" and the reply was: "It doesn't work like that, Ken, doesn't work like that." I can't remember who said it. Dad wouldn't have done that, no, he would not have been a party to anything like that. For example, he was one of the few who stood up to Bernie [Ecclestone]. He used to stand up to Bernie in meetings and Frank [Williams] always admired him for that.'

After the non-season of 1984, Brundle and Bellof stayed for 1985, the team totalled seven points and Bellof was killed driving a Porsche at Spa in a sports car race: an accident of immense ferocity into Eau Rouge as he tried to overtake another car. Years later, various people within Formula 1 were asked to nominate their candidate for the driver with the most unrealised potential, and Tyrrell selected Bellof. It hit him very hard.

In 1986, Brundle partnered Frenchman Philippe Streiff and the team finished with 11 points. At the end of that year Brundle departed to join the German team Zakspeed in what amounted to a swop with Jonathan Palmer.

'Ken was a very, very straightforward guy,' Palmer says, 'although not in the first dealings I had with him! That was 1984 when I was trying to get into Formula 1. I was Formula 2 Champion and obviously desperate to get into Formula 1. Martin Brundle was Formula 3 Champion, Senna had gone to Toleman, Martin was being talked about for Tyrrell along with Bellof – but having won Formula 2 I thought I should be higher up the pecking order than the guy who'd won the Formula 3 championship. I was banging on Ken's door – I didn't live too far away. I think Jackie [Stewart] had been involved with Martin to an extent and there was a link there, and there had been a bit of a gravitational pull towards Brundle driving for Ken. I could see it being positioned.

'I was asking Ken increasingly blunt questions. "Are you going to sign Martin Brundle? Have you signed Martin Brundle?" He said: "No, no, no." Subsequently I didn't believe him. Maybe I was asking some blunt questions that he particularly didn't want to answer, but at the end of the day, when push came to shove, he told me no, he hadn't signed him. Ironically, it was three years on that Martin had finished his three-year contract and we did the swop.

'That year in '87, I was very pleased to join Tyrrell because it was, I felt, a chance to drive for a proper team. Zakspeed had had a lot of enthusiasm but not the understanding, pedigree, background and common sense of Ken. I have to say that Ken was always very, very fair. He was never misleading to me – to the extent that sometimes I wish he had been! I had an option on my contract which ran out on the last day of November each year. At the end of 1987 I couldn't believe it. I'd won the championship for normally aspirated cars[1] and I said: "Can I assume, Ken, that I'm on for next year?" He said: "No, you can't assume anything." Then, a day before the option

Brundle and Bellof stayed with Tyrrell into 1985 and looked a very strong, fast young partnership. Bellof (no 4) was fourth at Detroit but Brundle (lower left) crashed (both Phipps/ Sutton). Bellof making a point to Lisles (lower centre) in Germany – about lack of power at a power circuit? He'd finish eighth, a lap behind the winner, Alboreto in a Ferrari (Schlegelmilch). Frenchman Philippe Streiff (lower right) partnered Jonathan Palmer in 1987 (Phipps/Sutton).

expired, I had a quick phone call. "Hello Jonathan. We're taking it up." "Jolly good, thanks, Ken." "Bye, then." He never took up the option any earlier than he had to, and when he did take it up he was courteous, but to the point.

'He'd been through a lot of motor racing, he was massively experienced and he didn't make huge amounts of money out of it. Probably he wasn't commercially astute enough to do that and there wasn't the sort of money around that there would be in the 1990s, so he'd had it pretty hard. He'd seen drivers come and go, he'd seen drivers being killed – a bit like Frank Williams. Those two were quite similar in their terseness in getting to the point and ruthlessness in what they are doing. They didn't let sentiment and emotion get in the way of running a business – and it's a business which has emotion oozing out of every pore if anyone wants to express that. They had a very

Jonathan Palmer finished fifth at the 1987 Monaco Grand Prix, a result which delighted Tyrrell (Phipps/Sutton).

different, hard approach to the whole thing, but at least you knew exactly where you stood.

'Ken was at his most animated talking about football or cricket. Whenever you were at a race meeting, the thing that would light up his face was seeing the cricket score or what happened in the football. I think that was his escape – but on the racing side he was certainly very blunt about things. I don't think however we ever rowed in the time that I was with the team. I don't remember having a falling-out with him.

'I did feel the team was going somewhere. The first year it was exciting for me because our aspirations were to win the Jim Clark Trophy [see Footnote 1] and although there were only seven cars in it, it was not uncompetitive, it was still a tough battle. And, particularly at the street circuits, we were competing for overall results as well. Finishing fifth at Monaco [as Palmer did] was a great achievement – but for me, when I think about it, the excitement was just finishing Grands Prix. I'd been with Zakspeed and RAM for so many years and there I did not expect to finish a Grand Prix because the cars weren't that reliable. When I joined Tyrrell, all of a sudden I was in a car with a team that actually expected to finish. We had the occasional mechanical glitch but it wasn't very often. In 1988 I had

expectations but that was a disappointment – the new car was late being produced, and it wasn't a good car.'

In 1988, Palmer would be partnered by Julian Bailey – and Bailey brought money with him, his own. 'The interesting thing about the money was that I sold the pub my brother and I owned in Hertfordshire,' Bailey says. 'I had some sponsorship – I think about £200,000 – but I had to give Ken half a million pounds. I said to him: "Well, I'm going to sell my pub" and that'll be the other £300,000. He said: "No, no, no, I'm not taking your money. You have to get it through sponsors." It was very strange. At the end I sold the pub anyway, gave the money to the sponsor and he gave it to Ken so Ken thought it all came from the sponsor.

'He struck me as very straight. Also, unless it was social, he was very minimalistic as far as the use of words went, a bit like Bernie [Ecclestone]. He's just say the minimum, but with maximum impact. He phoned me up once and said: "What day do you want to go to Japan? Wednesday or Thursday?" I said: "Thursday" and he put the phone down. That was it, that was all he wanted to know.

'I had no doubt about his love of the sport. There was quite a bit of a family atmosphere there because Norah was doing the catering. She would go: "Here's your ham sandwich without tomato – that one's Julian's." She'd go out and buy the bread, make the sandwiches. He was obviously on a bit of a tight budget. I said to him at one Grand Prix – I think it was in Brazil, where it was very hot and all the other teams had air-conditioned units – "Why haven't we got one?" He said: "You can have one – if you want to pay for it!"'

Take someone like Ron Dennis. He nurtures the drivers, he brings them on. 'I think Ken was just a bit harder. Obviously I was only with him for a year but I got on a lot better with him when I wasn't driving for him – because he had never done anything wrong to me and I had never done anything wrong to him. We had both fulfilled our sides of the bargain. I gave him the money, he gave me the car, I drove the car. And at the end, that was it. He used to take my boys to Tottenham sometimes and funnily enough I ended up living about five doors away from him in West

Clandon. It was just co-incidence that I happened to move there. I saw him occasionally, not very often because he was not the sort of bloke who would be in the local pub all the time. Bob lived the other side of me so I'd see him sometimes as well. Norah and I always got on well. We had a mutual like for each other, I think.'

Do you think he knew you'd just be there for one year and then he'd find somebody else – and therefore there was no point in getting close to a driver because he'd be gone?

'He'd been in the business a long time and I think he was unaffected. He'd had good friendships with drivers before – Alboreto was a good friend, although I don't know how that ended. It was somewhat acrimonious when he left. Alesi got on well with him. And once Jackie Stewart's been there you can never be anything but not as good as Jackie, can you?'

But you can't go on living on that 20 years later.

'He managed to somehow, didn't he?'

At Brazil, the very first time out in the car, you went out without a wing mirror.

'Both of them fell off! He said: "You shouldn't be looking behind you, you should be looking where you're bloody going." Prost and Piquet, they all came down the garage. It was a bit embarrassing for me because I had Prost and Piquet outside the garage wanting to have a word with me about my standard of driving when I couldn't see

where I was bloody going. Ken said to Piquet something like: "I remember your first race, you were crap as well." Didn't really help me, did it?'

That's the sort of thing Ron Dennis would never say.

'Well, he wouldn't let you out without mirrors on, would he?'

At Monaco, Palmer would be fifth again. 'Julian Bailey and I went testing at Croix-en-Ternois [a circuit in northern France] and the car seemed reasonably OK,' Palmer says. 'They'd done a long-wheelbased version but I thought the short-wheel had better traction. That was duly how we started to qualify at Monaco. Then – fortuitously – my car developed a gearbox problem and I had to jump in the spare. That was the long-wheelbased, improvised job and I was instantly about a second quicker. I was ninth on the grid and within one session we'd gone from struggling for 16th-17th place to the top ten.

'Monaco meant so much to Ken and fortunately I had my best results there. I think one of the reasons I was particularly good at Monaco was that it was such a demanding, action-packed go-go-go circuit that whatever natural talent I had came through unfettered without the mental overlay of over-thinking it. When I went to a faster circuit like Silverstone or Monza, and you'd sit on the straight for, say, 13 seconds I'd have too long to think about making the critical decisions. Whereas Monaco was

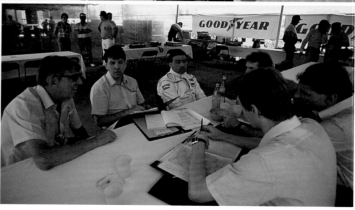

Left top: Streiff crashed at Monaco and may even have rung for a taxi (Phipps/ Sutton). Left: Julian Bailey went well when it rained, but qualifying at the 1988 Hungarian Grand Prix was dry and he didn't get into the race (Phipps/ Sutton). Top: The 1989 season started with Palmer partnering Alboreto, who had arrived from Ferrari as the great white hope (Phipps/ Sutton). At first there was harmony with Alboreto (above), but it didn't last to mid season (Phipps/Sutton).

one flurry of wild activity – more like rally driving. Ken loved it. Everyone loves Monaco, particularly if they do well, and it is always important for sponsors. Ken was always very good looking after the sponsors, and to go well there was very important. So Monaco was a boost, but 1988 generally was a pretty tough year. The exciting bit was at the end of that year when Ken wanted to make some changes, and he recruited Harvey Postlethwaite and Jean-Claude Migeot.'

Bailey was leaving.

Did you feel during the season that the relationship got strained?

'It was as it was all the way through and then it ended, in Australia after the last Grand Prix,' Bailey says. 'I said to him: "Well, what about next year?" and he said: "I don't know." It was pretty obvious that I wasn't going to be back in the team, and by this time Alboreto had come on the scene. He had backing from some Swiss bloke, some count. Palmer stayed, and he'd done a pretty good job that year – fifth at Monaco – but he had 80 Grands Prix behind him. I'd only done a couple of 3000 races as well as the 1988 season. Ken told me he wasn't taking up the option. He sort of said: "Well, that's it." It was matter of fact: that's business, you know. He was trying to survive in a very harsh environment without any sponsors, really, so he had to do whatever he had to do to keep the thing going. And that's a fact of life. If I'd had five million quid I'd probably have still been there.

'Ken was an interesting bloke, I really did like him but most of all I admired his honesty, his integrity. He would not lead you up the garden path. He'd say yes or no and I preferred it that way. You knew where you stood with Ken, and always did. I used to enjoy having dinner with the guy and he was funny, told some good stories.'

Palmer stayed, to be partnered in 1989 by Michele Alboreto – from Ferrari. As Palmer attests, with Postlethwaite, Migeot and Alboreto 'the team had high expectations. The game had been raised substantially. The second race at Imola, Alboreto had the new car. He was clearly a bit of a 'find' having been a Ferrari race winner. I got the old car but that made me almost more determined

because although I thought it wasn't fair, I was going to prove what I could do. As it happened, I ended up qualifying and Alboreto failed to qualify. Alboreto was a talented driver but also Italian and emotional. If he had a mental downer on something it would spiral down and down. He felt the new car was nervous, couldn't get on with it and thought it was fundamentally flawed.

'He seemed to go through the two practice and two qualifying sessions, as there were then, convincing himself and everybody around him that the new car was wrong. As a result it was a pretty gloomy Postlethwaite, Migeot and Ken. So they said: "Do you want to take over the new car for the race?" I thought: sure, I can't do any worse – I'd qualified 25th. The [Sunday morning] warm-up was my first time in it. I did a few laps and it felt amazingly 'pointy' – a lot of over-steer – and that's what put Alboreto off. It was so darty and sharp. But once you got used to it you realised it wasn't going to over-steer and in that warm-up I was eighth. It was clear to me that this car had loads more grip and straight line speed, so it was much better aerodynamically.

'I made an adjustment to the roll bar on the grid, started the race and worked my way up. It was just the most wonderful Grand Prix. Finally I was driving a car that had the straight line speed and the cornering grip. I was actually racing other cars and did overtake quite a few. To finish sixth was almost fairy tale stuff. Ken was delighted, absolutely delighted. What was wonderful was seeing the expressions of Harvey and Migeot – they were down in the mouth in a big way after qualifying and maybe thought the car did have a fundamental flaw. To see that it hadn't was a godsend to them and they were elated. By mid-season in Montreal I'd got the upper hand and I outqualified him comprehensively. It was after that race that he left the team.'

France was next and Alboreto was in open dispute – at the public level, anyway – with Tyrrell over a conflict of tobacco sponsors. Tyrrell now had Camel, Alboreto had Marlboro and the twain did not meet, they parted. 'I think,' Palmer says, 'that Alboreto came in to dominate and, when he didn't, he couldn't take it.'

Eddie Jordan, running Jean Alesi in Formula 3000, saw

everything all in the moment and, a moment after that, was at the timber yard with Alesi.

'I first met him in the factory the week before the race,' Alesi says. 'I have to say I was very impressed, because I arrived with Eddie Jordan and we went into Ken's office to say hello, obviously, and then Ken said: "OK, go for the seat fitting while I speak to Eddie about the contract." I was without words, I was blocked because he was such a hero for me.

'Then we went to Ricard but he'd told me what to do. He called me and said: "Look, it is very tough competition, some drivers may not qualify but you don't have to have pressure – just try to learn everything and don't crash because if you keep on going you will learn a lot." He made my feelings really cool, you know, because I had a lot of tension just before the first session at Ricard, especially because it was the first time in Formula 1 for me. At the end of the day I qualified seventh and he was really impressed and happy. I remember his smile!'

Jean Alesi arrived at the 1989 French Grand Prix, happy to make his F1 début – he left even happier, with a fourth place finish (Phipps/Sutton). Alesi moves to fourth place against the mighty backdrop of Jerez. This is the 1989 Spanish Grand Prix. (Phipps/Sutton)

You went out to dinner with Ken and Norah and you felt they were the best couple you had ever met in your life.

'Exactly. For such an unbelievable life, during all this time in Formula 1, and having a lot of success, being close to Norah like that and loving her – from the outside it was very easy to feel it.'

Alesi finished the French Grand Prix fourth, and at one stage, while the pit stops were going on, ran second. In 1 hour 39 minutes and 42.643 seconds he had launched a career which endured until 2001. After the race the awning outside the Tyrrell motorhome was a centre of attention in the way it hadn't been for years. Tyrrell beamed and guffawed and, stooping, spoke to Alesi in English. Whether Alesi understood wasn't clear because he kept nodding his head in a reflex action. Alesi did not seem at all surprised by being fourth and maintained his composure while a dozen journalists wanted interviews and a French TV crew hove into view headed doggedly towards him.

That Alesi had something about him was confirmed in Hungary, and an incident Tyrrell often recounted with a certain relish. Nigel Mansell felt Alesi had baulked him and advanced down the pit lane seeking an apology. Tyrrell told Alesi this and said that, whatever Alesi had or had not done, the easiest way out of the predicament was to offer the apology – and Mansell would go away. Tyrrell waited for Alesi's view of this, and Alesi took his time weighing it up. Then he said: "No, I don't think I want to do that" – and didn't. This delighted Tyrrell because, if you're going to make it in Formula 1, that's how you have to be.

'Yes, it's true,' Alesi says, reflecting and chuckling. 'It was in Budapest.'

The incident happened in Friday's first qualifying: Mansell (Ferrari) saw a yellow flag and immediately slowed, as the regulations stipulated. Alesi assumed Mansell was baulking him and, when they came towards the pit entrance, darted ahead and led Mansell down the pit lane very slowly indeed. Mansell was angry, and understandably so.

Ken Tyrrell didn't mind in the least. He'd found a gem.

I asked Palmer about leaving the team.

'Alesi had come in and Alesi out performed me. Within three races he was quicker than I was and I recognised this. The fact is that he was much younger and hungrier and prepared to take risks, all the classical things in a driver reaching Formula 1. I don't think Ken simply told me – it was becoming obvious. There wasn't an option situation because my contract was running out. If he's not saying you're staying you're getting a message.'

Palmer retired while Alesi stayed for 1990 with Satoru Nakajima to partner him.

'Before Alesi came,' Palmer says, 'I had a number of teams talking to me seriously, but of course all that fizzled out very quickly. At the start of 1989 I thought I was finally on the verge of making it through to the big time and winning a Grand Prix for a top team. Then the pendulum swung totally the other way.'

Looking back, what are your reflections on Ken Tyrrell now?

'He was somebody very special for a number of reasons. First of all, you can't do anything but admire the success that he had in Formula 1. He came from outside the sport from a family which didn't play any significant role in introducing him to it, he came in as a timber merchant, knew what he liked, loved the racing, was sensible enough to see what he wasn't going to achieve as a driver and moved across to team management. That pragmatic approach was something that he respected in drivers, too. He didn't like dreamers. He was very down-to-earth, very sensible in that way. He'd had a triple world champion with Stewart. It's a great name and I was always very proud to drive for Tyrrell. People knew Tyrrell. It was a team that had achieved. When I was there I always felt that the comeback was going to happen soon. I didn't think it was a down-and-out team and I'll just see what I can get out of it. I really believed that the comeback could be round the corner and with a few good breaks the team could move up. I could grow with it and succeed with it.

'It was always good fun being with the team. Although Ken was blunt, he'd be good company around the motorhome and he was very loyal and supportive, too. He might give you a hard time but you know he'd stand up for you if somebody else came along and said: "Isn't it about time you got Palmer out?" He might have his own private thoughts, and almost certainly did, but you never got the feeling that he was looking over his shoulder and doing you down. He was a straightforward guy and if you had a problem he'd tell you – and you'd hear it from him, not from somebody else.'

So Palmer went at the end of 1989 while Alesi was poised to throw Grand Prix racing into a convulsion – of delight.

NOTE:
[1] In 1987, turbo cars were dominant to such an extent that the seven drivers with non-turbo cars had their own championship within the World Championship itself. It was called the Jim Clark Trophy and Palmer won it with 87 points from Streiff (74) and Philippe Alliot (Lola) 43.

Chapter Eight

HOLDING ON

'He hadn't done a froth job for years. In the old days, if you remember, he did but for some reason – I don't know why – he stopped about 15 years ago.'

Bob Tyrrell

'It wasn't a fortune but I got paid on the dot. I'll say that for Ken: when he said he was going to do something he did it.'

Mark Blundell

'Having to participate rather than compete has not been easy. It causes rage, which is difficult to contain.'

Harvey Postlethwaite

Alesi was passionate, impulsive, emotional – just the man for a convulsion. In the United States Grand Prix at Phoenix, a street circuit, he qualified on the second row and reflected many years later that the Tyrrell 018 was either the best or one of the best cars he'd ever driven. At the start of the race he pitched the Tyrrell into the lead. Ayrton Senna, initially fourth, worked his way up to Alesi by lap 33 and, into lap 34 at the 90° right-hander after the pits, went down the inside to take the lead for himself – but the impetus of the move meant that the McLaren was pitched off-line and he had to get it back. They were surging towards the next corner, a 90° left and Alesi pitched the Tyrrell to the inside for that. He had the lead back from a move of instant reaction and . . . barefaced cheek. Inevitably, Senna regained the lead later, but Alesi harried him and finished only 8.6 seconds behind.

This is what Alesi says: 'Frightened of Senna? I had a lot of respect, you know, for all these kind of drivers because it was a time when the drivers were really important and you

The old master, Brazil, 1994 (Schlegelmilch).

had Mansell, Senna, Piquet and Prost. They were all heroes. I was fourth on the grid, I think, and I had a very good start – I led the race straight away. In my mind immediately I said: "I hope I am going to finish the first lap leading" because at least I'd be able to say I'd led a Grand Prix for one lap with my small car. When I say small car that means a small team and a small environment compared to Ferrari and McLaren and Williams. We were really small with Ken.

'Everything went very well and I was pushing-pushing-pushing and going away, and that was a great time. I concentrated very much to do the best and when Senna caught me I said: "OK, he is going to overtake me, there is no doubt about that, but I will not make things very easy." So that's why I had this opportunity to overtake him back – and I did it. I braked very late and he waited to brake – so

he braked even later and he had no chance to make the corner smoothly. And I caught him at the exit. I was sure I wouldn't be able to overtake him again after that because he was far and away the best driver and he watched every move, learnt every move. For sure he did one mistake – into the corner – but not two. So I'd retaken him. He said to himself, "OK, next time I will do it differently." And he did.'

Do you think, looking back, you were really the last chance that Ken had in terms of a driver capable of winning races?

'First of all, it's difficult to say that, difficult to say that he had no chance any more because you never know what can happen.'

You were second in Monaco . . .

'Because we did so well in Phoenix we were expecting to be quick in Monaco and we were quick. I was third in qualifying: Senna, Prost and myself. Then pushing very hard during all the race gave me second. That was again a great time but much more difficult than Phoenix, because in Phoenix, nobody expected much – even me – and in Monaco everybody was expecting it. So I had to do it – and I did it. But that was very tough because Monaco is not easy, not at all. And Ken loved Monaco!'

Alesi hounded Prost and on lap 31 Prost retired, an electronics failure. Alesi was 17.5 seconds behind Senna and towards the end eased off so that he only beat Alesi by 1.087 seconds.

What did you make of Tyrrell as a man?

'A great father, you know. The way he was helping the driver was as a father: not as a team manager or as a businessman. You never felt the business when you were with him. Never.'

Passionate, impulsive, emotional – yes. Listen to Bob Tyrrell. 'One of the problems with Jean was that what he loved most was the all-balls-out qualifying lap and there were times when you wanted to see how the race car was going to be. And he'd come in after one lap! Dad would make him go out and do it again – you'd tell him and it didn't make any difference. If you said: "We need a fast lap" he'd be wonderful but, time and time again, dad would say to him: "Jean, you understand?" and Jean would say "yes" and then he'd go out and forget all about it.'

Nakajima, who'd come from Lotus, was widely regarded as a gateway to the lucrative Japanese market and perhaps Honda engines. Nakajima was also a chirpy little chap who didn't make trouble. He'd stay a couple of seasons and during this time I was writing a profile of him for a Tokyo publishing company. I travelled down to the timber yard to interview Tyrrell, who was suitably diplomatic. 'I'm not going to say he'll win Grands Prix or championships, and don't expect me to, even though you're writing for his home audience. I will say that he is a good addition to the team in many ways.'

It was just the truth, and after Nakajima had stopped driving for Tyrrell he stayed close to the team.

In 1991, Tyrrell did get Honda engines. Tyrrell once showed me a photograph of the first engine flown over from Japan to the factory. When they uncrated it they found it was wrapped in ribbons and bows – our present to you. It touched Tyrrell a great deal.

Although Alesi had gone to Ferrari (inevitably, being French Sicilian and boiling with Latin blood), Nakajima stayed, to be joined by Stefano Modena. A problem was

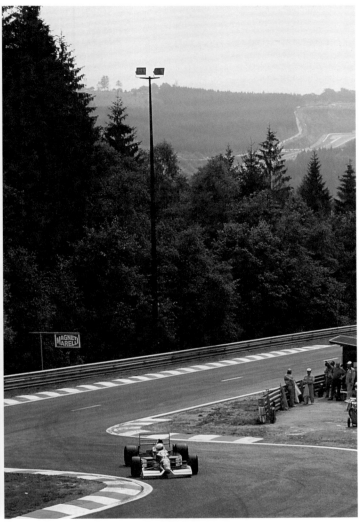

that McLaren had been triumphant with Honda engines since 1988 and were not anxious to see that diluted.

In 2002, I wondered to Bob Tyrrell if, in the team's long descent, there had been times when they could have reversed it. Bob was after all in charge of sponsorship, and a team can't exist without that. 'Particularly after we'd pulled out [in 1998] we used to talk about it a lot. We weren't clever enough in the latter years. I'd say "I was never able to get enough money in" and he'd say: "Yes, but

we were never able to make the car competitive."

'We almost broke out of it twice. The first time was when we had the Alesi 018 car, when we'd just got Harvey.' Postlethwaite[1] had in fact come to Tyrrell in 1990, although another designer, Jean-Claude Migeot, 'was largely responsible for that. It was more Migeot than Harvey on the aerodynamics.' Tyrrell had attracted a major sponsor, Braun, and it did seem that finally they could break out.

'In order to get the Honda engine McLaren wanted us to tie up with them. They did all our sponsorship. If they were going to let the Honda engine go somewhere else they wanted to have a degree of control over what happened.' McLaren got the new Honda V12 and Tyrrell the V10 with which McLaren had won the 1990 championship. 'It was very heavy, but again, we were all set up and looking good. Satoru had a lot of Japanese sponsorship, so for the first time – although we were paying for the engines – we had a good budget.

'We had made a fundamental error. In 1990, when we didn't have a good budget, we signed up with Pirelli tyres – a two-year contract. We should have done one year. The Goodyear tyres were going to cost $1.5m or whatever it was. Pirelli was nothing – sponsor's name on the car, that was it. We were making these kind of decisions. You have to ask: how did we let ourselves get into the situation? We'd obviously done things wrong. Then we were in a very good situation with the Honda engine, but the car never performed as well as 019 did and the Pirelli tyres were no good on all the fast circuits. I remember Braun coming to us and saying "We're not happy with this. My chairman keeps ringing up and saying we are sponsoring a team and where were they?"

'I don't think dad was concerned about the pressure from the sponsors. He took pressure pretty well. He hadn't done a froth job for years. In the old days, if you remember, he did but for some reason – I don't know why – he stopped about 15 years ago.'

Postlethwaite left in July to join Mercedes and that affected team morale. Modena finished the season eighth on ten points, Nakajima joint 15th on two. For 1992, Tyrrell lost the Honda engine and had Andrea de Cesaris and Olivier Grouillard as drivers. From there, somehow, the years would drift by – 8 points in 1992; none in 1993 (de Cesaris and Ukyo Katayama). Katayama, even more chirpy and cheerful than Nakajima, spent 1993 struggling with a disappointing Tyrrell chassis despite having a

Story of a season 1991 . . . Opposite: Nakajima (no 3) in the corkscrew final corner at Magny-Cours. The gift-wrapped Honda engine. Stefano Modena (no 4) in Japan. This page: Modena in Australia.

Yamaha V10 engine. Tyrrell believed that if Japan would ever produce a World Champion, Katayama was that man, and told me so forcibly. I mention this because he did not say such things lightly and you have seen his diplomacy over Nakajima.

In 1994, Mark Blundell came to partner Katayama.

THE DRIVER'S STORY, PART FIVE – Blundell had spent two seasons in Grand Prix racing, 1991 with Brabham and 1993 with Ligier.

'I knew Ken from getting into Formula 1 in the early days – obviously he was well known and well respected. Basically I had come away from Ligier on the basis that they really didn't want to have anybody who wasn't French speaking, and there were a lot of political things going on with government-backed sponsors and so on. The situation was there with Tyrrell. I didn't have any sponsorship, which in those days Tyrrell wanted desperately, but they took me on merit and paid me. It wasn't a fortune but I got paid on the dot. I'll say that for Ken: when he said he was going to do something he did it and there was no waiting around for your money. When it said in your contract you got it, you got it, and always on the nail.

Andrea de Cesaris joined in 1992 and provided an image of Monaco we know well. (Sutton). Things rarely went well for de Cesaris – throughout his career (Sutton). Mark Blundell (right) looking serious in 1994. He would put Tyrrell back on the podium in Spain (Sutton).

'I found him easy to get along with because there were similarities and parallels between us. He was a straight talker. He said what he said and you knew where you stood. I much prefer that than the other way. In that year Ken was starting to wind down slightly. You could see it: Bob was taking more of a front seat in terms of what was going on. Ken hadn't reached the back seat – he was in a sort of middle seat because he still had a lot of input and the final say in many areas.'

Katayama finished fifth in Brazil, Blundell crashed; neither finished in the Pacific Grand Prix at Aida, Japan; Katayama was fifth at San Marino, Blundell ninth, and all meaningless in Senna's shadow; neither finished at Monaco. Barcelona was quite different.

'We had been showing great speed in many, many areas although in some ways I was up against it because Ukyo weighed nothing and was Yamaha's golden boy although I was also held in high regard by them because I'd scored their first World Championship points [with Brabham] and now their first podium. Ukyo was about eight stone and I was 11.2 – you'd get the speed graphs out and you could see the difference, although some of that was his engine spec., which was slightly different to mine. That's understandable now, but maybe it wasn't then.'

Blundell finished third at Barcelona, albeit 1m 26.969s behind the winner, Damon Hill (Williams).

'The third place came pretty much because we stayed to the end of the race, that's how you have to look at that one. We kept our heads down and stayed. Ken took it in the way you'd expect. He enjoyed it from the team's perspective. If you're in the position where your performance is what it had been and you've got an engine manufacturer and you've got sponsors there, when you do pull something off it's all welcome and all needed. We should have had a few results. Monza we were running very, very quickly and unfortunately ran out of brakes . . .

'The intentions were that we were going to try to stay together but circumstances decided otherwise. It was purely driven by finance: they needed sponsorship and I didn't have it. We worked for as long as we could trying to make things happen and I held out for quite a long time but in the end I could wait no longer and they had to make their decisions as well. They were very straightforward about it: you know, life's life, we have to go on and we've got employees who we need to make sure get through our door every day.

'They had the motivation that they could go somewhere if they could get an engine deal and if they could get a sponsor. If is F1 backwards – a small word with a huge meaning, and they never did pull off the big money and the big engine manufacturer. Yamaha did not have the resources of a Honda or a Renault and although Harvey was there [he returned in this season of 1994] and Mike Gascoyne[2] was there it still wasn't operating at the level it needed to.'

In 1995, Katayama stayed, to be partnered by Mika Salo and then Gabrielle Tarquini.

Chris Leslie joined that year in purchasing, which 'means anything and everything that needs to be bought. We were buying toilet rolls one minute and carbon fibre the next and gearbox parts the minute after that.' He stresses that the team never felt they were going nowhere, 'never felt like that at all. All everyone thought was: "What we need is money and/or an engine. Maybe with the engine we can get the money or with the money we can get the engine." We were all totally convinced that we had the people to do it. Everyone was behind Ken and we were priveleged to be working there as opposed to the other teams, because they were becoming big business. We almost judged that that wasn't racing any more. Yes, it was going to be a struggle but we did feel all we needed was the engine. The morale at the team was fantastic.'

The money? Ah the damned, elusive money. Bob Tyrrell explains that through those lean years the Tyrrell team did not nearly go bust, 'no, because we always managed to solve it by cutting back – which of course is the last thing that you should be doing. We looked at everything. If any personnel wanted to go Club class they had to pay for it themselves. So Harvey and I and dad were all paying passengers if we did want to go Club. You look at how many want to fly to the races and you're saving maybe quarter of a million a year. And that didn't happen in Formula 1 – they've all got private aircraft, helicopters and all this sort of thing.'

Ken Tyrrell would not countenance debt, or unpaid bills, nor – in a pursuit like Formula 1 of ultimate extravagance – living beyond his means. It was, as Bob concedes, the old-fashioned way – and if anybody can find a better alternative, I'd like to see it.

And the years drifted: in 1996 Tyrrell ran Katayama and Salo (Salo five points, Katayama nil); for 1997 Katayama went and so did the Yamaha engines, to be replaced by the Ford V8. Salo and Jos Verstappen drove, both were seen as fast young men but between them the sole points finish – fifth, Salo at Monaco – suggested a vulnerable team. In June the rumours began, that Craig Pollock (manager of Jacques Villeneuve) was part of a consortium – cigarette company BAT and racing car manufacturer Reynard were also in it – negotiating to buy Tyrrell.

By now, Tyrrell, Williams and McLaren were locked in a dispute with Bernie Ecclestone over, essentially, who owned Formula 1 and how much they got from Ecclestone's company, which owned the TV rights and which he wanted to float.

'No way did dad want to sell the team,' Bob Tyrrell says, 'but he stood up for what he believed to be right. Bernie was going to float his company and we were standing out for our share and we couldn't understand that the others weren't. Ron [Dennis] and Frank [Williams] are honourable. The other teams got together and said: "Right, well these three teams aren't here so we'll divide the money amongst us." We're talking the TV money, basically. Instead of dividing it by ten you divided it by seven. Dad would never have done that. He would have said: "It's not right. We've got to sort it out, we need to sort it out."

'Anyway, it had a serious affect because it meant we were getting trickles of income coming through, that led to some difficulties and we had to be very, very, very careful. We never once ended up with no money in the bank. Never. We never had debts. You hear of teams with debts of £20 million. We would have closed down rather than do that.'

This is no place to go into the complexities of Ecclestone's float. Suffice to say that in Bob Tyrrell's words 'the whole thing dragged on and we couldn't afford for it to drag on. We took the decision when BAT came to see us and we started a dialogue. In fact we had some other discussions going on at the same time, not about selling the company but about getting an engine. The engine thing didn't come to fruition and by then we faced the question: do we got for it and try to make it work – or not? A difficult decision. Dad didn't want to do it [sell], it was like pulling teeth. He said to me subsequently that we did the right thing, but at the time it was hard.'

That was November 1997 and Ken Tyrrell insisted he

In Canada Blundell spun off, and in Hungary he took to the grass but finished the race fifth. Ken Tyrrell believed that if ever Japan was to produce a World Champion, it would be Ukyo Katayama, seen here in 1995, his third year with the team. Katayama goes off in qualifying at the 1995 Italian Grand Prix (all Sutton).

had chosen to sell rather than been forced to. He was past 70 and could have been forgiven for saying he'd had enough, but that wasn't the case at all; he disliked inactivity.

The price, never disclosed, was estimated at £20 million. He, Bob and Postlethwaite would remain in nominal control across 1998. Thereafter the team would be known as British American Racing (BAR). The uncertainty of who would go and who would stay cannot have helped. (Chris Leslie captures this uncertainty when he says 'at the end the Tyrrell team was 120 strong. BAR were talking about having eight or ten in the purchasing office, and we had two . . .')

The final drivers were Ricardo Rosset and Toranosuke Takagi. They did not score a point. The final race was Japan, 1 November. Rosset didn't qualify under the 107 per cent rule[3] and Takagi had a crash after 28 laps.

And that was it.

THE DRIVERS' STORY, FINAL PART – Rosset, Brazilian, had driven for Arrows in 1996 and once for Lola in 1997.

'I didn't have a lot of contact with Ken in 1998 because when I was driving there he was almost leaving the team, almost a guest at every race that he came to, not a team owner. We had a pleasant time, me and Ken. We never had any kind of problems but he wasn't actually involved in a way that he would have been if he'd been managing the team. I could feel he was sad because, in a way, by selling the team he was giving away a son.

'I think he saw at the time that the team was not being managed the way he would have liked it done but he had sold it so he had to live with it. He could almost feel that it was the end of his time as being part of motor racing. For me it was very difficult because it was a bit of a mess. There were a lot of things going on between the new team – Craig Pollock was not really worrying how the team performed because he was looking to BAR and the next year. That upset me because it was my chance and I needed to do well.

'On the other side we had Takagi, and there were a lot of people in the team pushing Takagi because they wanted to do the Honda deal [a projected Formula 1 team] so they wanted to make him look a very good driver compared to me. I didn't need to look good for them and therefore I didn't feel the team was behind me. I was coming back from the Lola thing, which was not very good as well, and this was my last chance really to show that I could do it. I did my best. I had a few accidents because I was pushing over the limit, but the car wasn't good and there was nobody I could talk to.

'The designers and so on were worried that they wouldn't stay on with BAR so they wanted the Honda deal. I was in the middle of these politics and I didn't have a good time.

'I didn't qualify for Tyrrell's final race in Japan because I had a problem with my neck in free practice. I pulled a muscle just driving, I didn't hit anything – maybe a bump or something. I heard something like a crack on my neck. That was Friday. So Saturday morning I couldn't move, my neck was really stiff and Suzuka is very hard on the neck. I didn't do the free practice in the morning because I went to the doctor, I spoke with Sid [Watkins] and he said: "We don't know if it's a muscle. It could be your spine, so you'd better have it checked before you get in the car." I went to the hospital at Suzuka and they did a scan on my neck. There was no problem with the spine, it was just the muscle. They said: "What do you want to do? We can inject you with some pain killers and you can try." I said: "As long as it's not a problem with my spine, do whatever you have to because I want to try and qualify." They gave me two injections on my neck, I went straight from there to the qualifying and I couldn't really drive the car because my neck still hurt.

'That was the last race of Tyrrell. I said goodbye to Ken and I said goodbye to everybody. I was very upset in the middle of the season because they were trying to push me out, and that was really bad. At the end everything was lost so I didn't want to have bad feelings about anybody. Ken wasn't part of it, as I say he was just a guest and I admired him. When I went to Tyrrell I felt honoured. I knew that Takagi and I were to be the last of the Tyrrell team that had made history in Formula 1. For me it was an honour to be part of that history and I wanted to do well, to end that history well – at least get a point. At the end of the year we had a picture of myself, Takagi, Jackie Stewart, all

The team of 1997 (back row, from left) chairman Ken Tyrrell, sporting director Satoru Nakajima, and engineering director Harvey Postlethwaite; (front row, from left) race driver Mika Salo, test driver Toranosuke Takagi and race driver Jos Verstappen (Avenue Communications).

Salo at Monaco in 1997, where he finished a superb fifth (ICN UK Bureau).
Opposite: The end. Ricardo Rosset fails to qualify for the team's final race, the 1998 Japanese Grand Prix (Sutton).

the team – and it was an honour to be part of that. Ken and his wife were good people.'

Postlethwaite, who'd take a goodly portion of the staff with him to the Honda project, said: 'Having to participate rather than compete has not been easy. It causes rage, which is difficult to contain.'

Let's end this chapter on a more human, and cheerful, note.

Charles Hewlett, who played football with Tyrrell for Ockham so long before, had been by profession a warehouseman at a Guildford company which sold motor parts. In those days, Hewlett says, Tyrrell 'had several vehicles for the timber business, including an old War Department Canadian Chevrolet, which had parts in common with Bedfords. We'd have a look and he'd say: "We'll make that do." He was always just the same. He'd have a load of timber on the truck outside or he'd have popped it in his car or whatever he had. He'd be in his working clothes. He was very generous to the British Legion. Every year he had a collection box up there at the firm and encouraged them all to put something in it. He put in it himself, too.

'I went up there saying "is it all right for the poppies again this year?" and he showed me round. It wasn't long before he made the decision to sell up. I was particularly interested in the components side, the stores and so on. He suddenly turned to me and asked what the part number was for a specific part for a specific Bedford. 'I said "905309 . . ."'

Guffaw.

NOTES:
[1] Dr Harvey Postlethwaite, one of the leading designers who had worked for Ferrari.
[2] Mike Gascoyne, from Norwich, studied engineering at Cambridge and joined McLaren as an aerodynamicist before, in 1991, working on chassis dynamics for Tyrrell.
[3] To qualify for a race, a driver must be within 107 per cent of the pole setter's time – a precaution to ensure that the disparity between the front and the back of the grid is not dangerously wide.

Chapter Nine

ELDER STATESMAN

'His enthusiasm could be over the top. If he went to the West End and saw a play he'd come back and say: "You've got to see this."'

Bob Tyrrell

'He said: "Well, what's your next thing?" I said, "a documentary on you" and he didn't really take it seriously. "Ah, you don't want to do that. Not interesting! Not important!"'

Mark Stewart

'The day he was going in for the operation he rang me and I said: "Ken, are you sure you are doing the right thing? London is near and America is just over the pond." He said: "DON'T START!"'

Sir Jackie Stewart

Evening at Silverstone in April 2000, some few days before the British Grand Prix, where, once upon a time, Ken Tyrrell bestrode the paddock dispensing wisdom and bonhomie. The giggle-gurgle-guffaw would echo out from the confines of the Tyrrell motorhome and invariably he'd be in animated conversation with someone or everyone. Across all these years, Grand Prix racing had been constructed on certain pillars and he was one. This April evening all that was memory.

Rain hung in the air and darkness wasn't far away, making the empty circuit seem even emptier except for the marquee opposite the new BRDC tower[1] where row after row of people sat waiting for what was called 'An Evening

If you can walk with kings and never lose the common touch. Silverstone, 1990. Tyrrell with the Duke of Kent and (now) Sir Jackie Stewart (Sutton).

With Ken Tyrrell'. He and we would watch the screening of a documentary about his career – made by Mark Stewart, son of Jackie – and afterwards give what in effect was an audience.

The film was called *Surviving Formula 1*, something appropriate enough. The film covered Tyrrell being given a special BRDC award at a London hotel and Stewart was saying 'Ken Tyrrell had that uniqueness, a very special fingerprint that he put on to the pad of motor racing.'

Tyrrell was, in fact, Mark's godfather and Norah his godmother. Mark says 'You can't in one breath say Ken without saying Norah. I was very proud to have had Ken as my godfather. Interestingly enough, anytime when I was with him – whether it be at a race where I was a guest – he'd take me round the paddock. At a race at Barcelona he was introducing me to people saying "this is my godson." He had a huge big grin. It was like he was almost proud of that. That sounds like conceit – but I was proud because ever since I was a child, when I started realising he was my godfather I always looked up to him. I also saw how my father looked up to him. And when they looked at each other it was always done in a nice way with a very friendly sparkle in their eyes, whether it involved business or pleasure. I noticed those things as a young boy.

A friend in high places. Tyrrell was not afraid to stand up to Bernie Ecclestone over the years, even though he respected him enormously (Phipps/Sutton, Schlegelmilch lower right).

'I loved motor racing, just as I love going to motor races. I love the smell. Remember those couple of years when they were using jungle juice?[2] What I liked about him, I'd go to a race and he'd say: "Mark, this is your home. Right? OK? This is where you come, you eat here." Anything you wanted, it was no problem. I would be in the back of the motorhome and he'd be having amazing conversations with somebody – quite serious stuff. When you went to the Tyrrell motorhome it was very simple, there was less money in it but you never got this "who are you, are you important enough?" Elsewhere that is understandable in some respects because some teams have too many people coming. I felt very much at home with Ken and Norah.

'The documentary? First of all, he didn't want me to make it. One thing Ken wasn't was greedy. He was an enthusiast. I had to convince him. I'll never forget – we were walking together and I said: "Ken, I'd love to make a documentary on you." He said "but what are you doing now, what's your next thing?" I said: "Well, a documentary on you" and he didn't really take it seriously. "Ah, you don't want to do that. Not interesting! Not important!" I don't think he realised until after the documentary that it was interesting and it was important. Murray Walker said: "If you go to your grave having not documented your life you've committed a crime!"

'I forgot it for a while – well, left it for a while then I went back and visited it again. "Ken, I really would like to do a documentary on you." Not only did he not want to do it, but people said to me: "Mark, it won't sell, he's not big enough," all that kind of stuff. I said to him: "Tell you what, if I make a pilot" – a pilot being a short film – "it will focus my mind and give you an idea of what we're going to try and do. We will also be able to see what other people think of the idea." So I made this pilot, he saw it, was rather taken by it – I think! – and said: "OK, I'll let you make the documentary." Then he said: "Do it for commercial reasons, do it to make money out of it. Don't lose money out of it." In truth, I wanted to do it because I wanted to do it. He thought I was wasting my time, completely wasting my time. He had no idea a TV broadcaster would be interested. It's been on all around the world, national TV here – ITV One, and it's available on videotape.

'Some things he didn't want to talk about. "Stay away from those things, we don't want to talk about them." An example: when they were taken out of the championship for the fuel tanks. He was still so angry. I talked to him about it off camera and he really felt cheated there. He liked the sport and he liked to compete and he felt it was disallowed because we have decided to disallow it. He said: "We don't want to do that because it'll get you in trouble, Mark. You don't want people to be looking down on you and saying Mark Stewart's got into trouble over a documentary." He was protecting me.

'It was interesting to see him reflect. I remember my

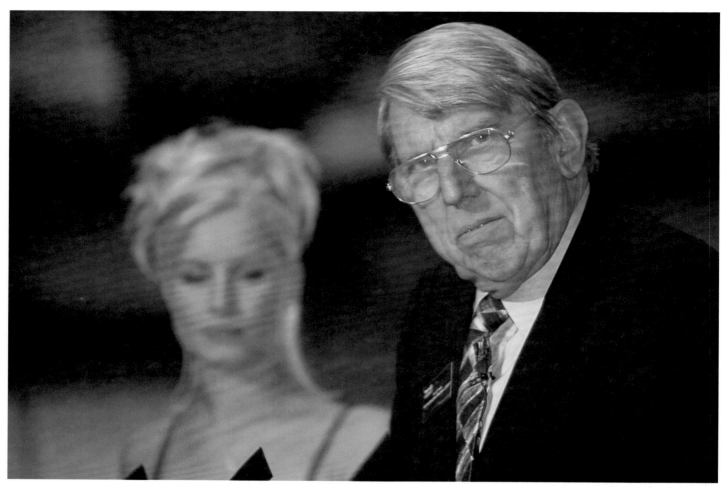

father told me that Ken called him after he'd seen the documentary and said firstly he liked it and he added "crikey, we really did do quite a lot! I've just realised how much – and how almost impossible it would be now."'

Jody Scheckter was there that night at Silverstone. I asked him to reflect on Tyrrell much, much later. 'I think Ken in his era was wonderful. They put a very family-orientated team together and that was fantastic. I admired and I loved Ken and in fact when I came back from America [where he'd been running a business] I got more and more friendly with him – more than it was when we were racing. In fact, my better recollection of Ken was the time I went

shooting with him and the time I spent with him in what proved to be the last days. [Scheckter moves subconsciously into the present tense.] He is one of the very few guys who is prepared to stand and get counted – and there is not many of them around. I can only love that in a guy. I repect that tremendously and I got very fond of Ken . . . '

Neil Davis reflects how Tyrrell misunderstand his own past and his own achievements. 'I was very friendly with Ken right up until his death. I used to go and visit him and we'd go shooting together. I knew Ken was completely against writing a book. I always said to him that he should but he dug his heels in and said "No." Unfortunately a lot of the information has gone with Ken, stories he had which will always be untold. A great shame, really.

'He never appreciated what he'd done. He had no interest in history: past was past and today is the future. It was quite incredible that he never kept any of his cars and it was fortunate one of the grandsons has bought 001 and kept it, but other than that there's nothing. Nothing. I mean, I went over with his son Kenneth and sorted out all the cups which were in Ken's loft. They'd been up there for God knows how many years – since the beginning. He just stuck them out of the way and he wasn't interested in any of them. There were some beautiful cups up there.'

Why do you think that was?

'I don't know, I don't know.'

Mind you, as Bob Tyrrell says, his 'enthusiasm could be over the top. If he went to the West End and saw a play he'd come back and say "you've got to see this."'

The innocence of pleasure, and the love of sport, may explain why Keith Boshier feels that the big business/big money aspect of Formula 1 'affected him – just a personal opinion. He never wanted to damage motorsport in any way whatsoever. Particularly towards the end he was very, very careful in what he said.'

He remained active for as long as it was physically possible. 'In November 2000,' Derek Daly says, 'there was a new initiative called Motorsport Ireland and I was the first recipient of their Hall of Fame. They asked Ken if he would present it and he said gladly. He was in Dublin to do that, which was a very, very nice gesture. I had not seen him for quite a long time and to me he was just the same. He told me all about his battle with cancer. He was happy to be active and he was just the same. We talked about all sorts of stuff and the conversation flowed immediately. There was no awkwardness and never had been with myself or Ken.'

Chris Leslie was with the Tyrrell team 'from 1995 to the bitter end on the purchasing side' also doing 'a bit of production work and logistics. When BAR took us over there were all sorts of negotiations – redundancies and so on – and I ended up being put forward to represent all the staff. I had to get a little bit closer to Ken and Bob.

'Then, when it was over, a load of us went with Harvey to the Honda project and through that – because we kept in close touch – I started running an unofficial Tyrrell Reunion Society or whatever you want to call it. It started off with really small get-togethers in pubs round East Horsley and that area. Ken was in the pub with us one day and we said: "We're thinking of having a Christmas dinner but not at Christmas because everyone's busy at Christmas – we'll have one in January just like we used to have." It would probably be small because there was only about 20 or 30 of us. Ken said: "Yes, I'd love to come", so it took off from there.

'Ken wasn't very well but he was well enough to come with Norah to that reunion. He said: "Chris, if you organise it I'll pay for it." I said: "Yes, all right, thank you very much" – but as we started saying to people: "Right, where shall we go?" more interest came in and suddenly I was getting phone calls from people I'd never heard of before who worked for Ken in the 1960s. The funniest thing was of course, as it grew, I had to ring Ken.'

Dialogue . . .

Leslie: 'We've got quite a few people now.'

Tyrrell: 'How many?'

Leslie: 'About 80 – about 80 with their other halves.'

Tyrrell: 'I'm not paying for other halves!'

Leslie: 'That's fine, no problem.'

A venue was found at Brooklands and then there was the matter of getting a disco organised.

Tyrrell: 'Disco?'

Leslie: 'Yes, Ken, just like our Christmas dinners. Got to have a disco.'

Tyrrell: 'I'm not paying for a disco!!'

'This,' Leslie says, 'went on and it was absolutely hilarious. True to his word he paid for every single ex-Tyrrell employee who was there.

'I would never claim to know him really well. I saw him very few times during the course of my working life. If he did come in it was very short and very sharp – not sharp but brief. He didn't waste time. "Can you organise this for me? Can you do this for me?" That was it. I got to know him

You handsome beast, you. Showbusiness person Denise van Outen isn't bad looking either (LAT).

better afterwards when we were doing these reunions. Again, because he was ill, it was a lot of "how are you doing?" He never dwelt on how ill he was.

'The party was at Goodwood in March 2001. Some of them hadn't seen each other since the 1970s or even the 1960s – in those days there was only four of them who travelled to the races. It was as if they'd got the whole team back together again under one roof for the first time since they'd left, and it was incredibly emotional. There were speeches and people kept going up to tell more and more stories. You'd hear these old guys talking about Stewart running over their foot at Monaco . . . '

To capture how Ken Tyrrell did think, and the sort of terrain his mind covered so easily, I propose to reproduce verbatim an interview he gave me the season after he'd retired. When I was arranging this on the phone, I ventured that he might be enjoying retirement. 'No – rather be working!' We met – where else? – in The Barley Mow and tucked ourselves into a corner of the dining room. He ordered a Guinness.

Monaco actually does attract celebrities. Pop star Cher tries the Tyrrell, which must have been about the equivalent of hearing Tyrrell sing (ICN UK Bureau).

Is there too much sport these days?

'No. There can't be too much sport. People have got so much more leisure time and sport soaks up some of that.'

When did you get into this?

'I started driving in 1952 and realised it wasn't for me in 1958. I drove Formula 3 at first and then graduated to Formula 2 and it was there that I started getting disappointed with things. One day I put a young guy in the car called Michael Taylor[3] and he went so well, and I got so much pleasure out of the car going well, that I thought this is what I must do.'

As a team owner, you were aware of the world outside Grand Prix racing and knew something about it.

'There's quite a well-known story of when we were at the Nürburgring and Jackie Stewart was driving for us. The car wasn't going very well in practice and he was moaning about it. I said to him: "You think you've got troubles, England are 88 for 4 against the Australians.!" I was only

trying to put things in perspective [chuckle].'

How has Grand Prix racing changed in the last 30 years?

'Well, it hasn't changed all that much, really. There's always been only two or three teams that can win a Grand Prix in any particular year, usually only two teams that can win the championship in that year and only one or two drivers. The major change since we started as a Grand Prix team in 1968 is that the cars are so much safer. I was at Watkins Glen early in 1998 to dedicate a plaque to François Cevert, who was killed there, and I went and had a look at the place where he had his accident. If he had been driving a 1998 car he would have walked away from it.

'So the biggest change is safety, and then of course the improvement in tyres: when we had slick tyres it gave us much more grip. And finally the aerodynamics.'

What about the commercial side? When you started, you could buy Cosworth engines and you went motor racing.

'It's true that that happened with the advent of the Cosworth engine, which made its début at Zandvoort in 1967 in the Lotus. I went over to watch that race and it was absolutely clear that here was the engine of the future – and it would be a good time to get into Formula 1. That engine dominated for about ten years, I suppose. In 1968 you'd go up to Cosworth at Northampton with £7,500 and you walked away with an engine capable of winning the next race if you had the right car with the right driver. That's long gone. You can't do anything like that today because, forgetting the cost, it is not possible for example to get the engine that Mika Häkkinen uses in the McLaren. You cannot go to Mercedes and say: "I want one of those no matter how much it costs!" They are not available'

What sort of a budget were you talking about in 1968?

'I can tell you exactly, but you've got to remember we didn't manufacture cars, we used a Matra – and the Matra was on free loan to us. They supplied the car, spare parts and one engineer. Our budget for '68 was £80,000.'

What about the financial pressures? You withstood them and they took teams under, including Lotus.

'It's not fair to include Lotus because they lost the man – Colin Chapman – and anything was likely to happen to it then. I mean, what would happen to McLaren if Ron

the sponsors bring in the money because of the TV and the enormous exposure that Formula 1 gets. And the man who is master at doing that is BE [Bernie Ecclestone].'

Has friendship between the teams and drivers declined?

'I think it might have somewhat. It used to be the case that teams borrowed bits and pieces from one another. If you hadn't got something you went along to another team and said: "Have you any?" Today you wouldn't ask. Also, we did use a lot of components on the car that were similar to those on other cars, and that's different today. There isn't much you could borrow: maybe clutch and the brakes, but even they get modified, so you wouldn't want to lend them.'

What's struck me over the years is that drivers don't really know each other very well. They seem to live in these little compartments. Was it better in the old days?

'I never believe that the old days were better. You cannot live in the past: there's no such thing as the good old days. Formula 1 has got better every year. There are various things wrong with it, there are always things you'd like to do if you were God, but it really does get better and better, employing more and more people for more and more money – so it's better for everyone who's working in it. And it's a very high-tech environment. I was a vice-president of Silverstone and they hadn't got the modern pit complex and everyone in FOCA [the Formula 1 Constructors' Association] at that time had a job. You'll be surprised to learn that Frank Williams's job was toilets! [chuckle] Some of them were appalling. Watkins Glen, certainly. The last time we were there and we knew we weren't going back, Bob Dance of Lotus blew them up [chuckle]. Anyway, I was given the job of telling Silverstone that unless they did something about the pits, the British Grand Prix would go to Brands Hatch . . . '

What aspect of Formula I are you missing most?

'Just being there. Just being part of it. Just being part of the decision making, being involved – what tyres are we going to use? What's the race strategy going to be? – everything that I used to do. So I sit and watch it on TV wondering if they're going for a soft tyre or a hard tyre, are they going to stop once or stop twice?'

You always saw the political crises within the sport in

Dennis wasn't there? OK, the teams are better organised but I'm not sure they'd continue doing what they're doing without the guiding light. We didn't go under because we only spent the money that we had, we didn't start spending the money that belonged to somebody else. That said, our workforce was 120 at the end – when we ran the Matra, OK, the car was provided but we actually ran it with six people, six or eight, that's all. Today you need 25 to 30 just running the car. All brought about, of course, by television:

terms of common sense. Is it as political as people suggest?

'Yes it is, and it's true that my approach to things was practical and down-to-earth because I am not a sophisticated person. Therefore I couldn't get involved in sophisticated arguments.'

And about the egos in it?

'We've all got egos. An example. When we finished first and second in Sweden with the six-wheeler it was a bit special. Luca di Montezemolo was the team manager at Ferrari and I liked him. At FOCA meetings he made decisions. After the race he came, got down on his knees in front of everybody and said: "Absolutely fantastic". He didn't have to do that, did he? [chuckle]. A few years ago at Imola I reminded him of it and he didn't remember [chuckle] – maybe his ego wouldn't let him! The first time we went to Argentina, Juan-Manuel Fangio very kindly took me round the track in his road car with an interpreter. Afterwards he said: "Ken, if you had been making cars at the same time that I was driving, together we could have made something." Good for my ego!'

Son Bob has inherited so much of his father's easy approachability, and seriousness. He was a senior team member for many years (Schlegelmilch).

Confining it to drivers, is it possible to be good without an ego?

'There is so much international coverage for successful sportspeople that it shows in some of them, but others can stand back and keep a level head. It's difficult for them.'

And you need self-belief, you need a bit of an ego.

'Absolutely. Take Martin Brundle. He has improved in the ordinary walks of life because of his tremendous success on TV.'

Is it going to be progressively more difficult for small teams to grow and evolve?

'Yes, because of the amount of money you need to actually start, and it's huge, so I find difficulty seeing how small teams can come in now.'

Unless you do it the Eddie Jordan way, bit by bit.

'But he was in a different era – seven or eight years ago, and it was still possible then. The Cosworth engine was quite competitive and he had a successful first year. It was relatively easy to make the car reliable – you didn't have these electronic gearboxes and so on – but now the only people who can do it are cigarette companies or a motor manufacturer like Honda. I'm afraid the days when teams could move up from Formula 3000 are long gone.'

What was the best moment of your career?

'I described it at a dinner the other day in front of a couple of thousand people at the Grosvenor House Hotel in London. Steve Rider was the compere and he asked me what was the highlight. I said: "For the last 55 years I've been waking up every morning with a beautiful naked woman [Norah] lying beside me [chuckle] . . ."

The best drivers of all time?

'I caught the end of Fangio, I saw Fangio drive but I always answer this question the same way: Fangio, Stirling Moss, Jimmy Clark, Jackie Stewart, Ayrton Senna – and now, I suppose, Schumacher.'

A final question: your view of the future?

'I'm pleased to hear that at last the FIA have been giving some consideration to a change in the cars which will allow overtaking to return, because we do need that. That apart, I think Formula 1 is going from strength to strength and I don't see anything standing in its way.'

As he spoke these words it never crossed my mind that they would prove to be almost the perfect epitaph.

When Sir Jackie Stewart heard that Tyrrell was ill, he moved quickly. 'There was nobody I should have done more for than him. I think I was able to give him an extra two years of quality life. If he'd caught it [had treatment for the cancer] earlier . . .

'The day he was going in for the operation he rang me and I said "Ken, are you sure you are doing the right thing? London is near and America is just over the pond." He said: "DON'T START!" He knew it was a cancer problem but he didn't know the scale and neither did the surgeon until he opened him up.'

Evidently it was so advanced as to be inoperable, although Stewart did not necessarily accept that.

'I had to get his two sons involved so he would pay attention to what I was saying. I had two doctors come to see him in London to say that he could be operated on. I

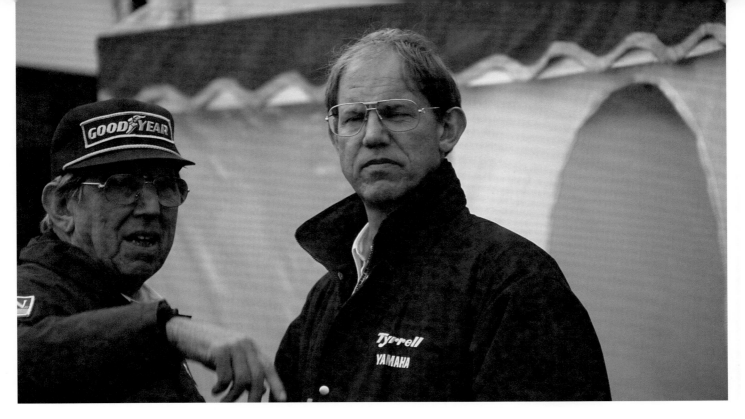

brought a surgeon over [from the States] who said: "I don't understand it – I did five of these last week."'

Stewart was buying time.

Mark Stewart went on to make a documentary about Sir Jackie and, although Tyrrell's health was visibly worse, he wanted to be part of it. 'After I'd made the documentary on him he realised the importance. He was very good talking about my father. There's a very touching moment with Ken when they were together in the woodshed [at the factory], the two of them sitting there. I filmed it from far away because of Ken's illness' – so people would not see how gaunt he had become. 'Even so he said: "Right, I'll do it."'

'I remember the last day we met and I knew it would be the last. This was at his house. We sat down and had the most incredible conversation. He was very ill, very ill. He was still as strong as an ox in his mind but he knew he was dying and he asked me to do a couple of things for him, following his death. It was a conversation I have never had in my life before with anybody. A great man. I loved him to bits, I miss him. Going away that last time I was very emotional about it. I was also very warmed by the fact that we had had the conversation that we did. He was angry, he

didn't want to go. He was upset to leave Norah behind and he didn't want to leave yet. I think he had accepted it at that point. He loved motor racing, loved Formula 1 and the thought of not being able to watch a race again or a football match, going down to Tottenham, that was difficult.'

The time which Jackie Stewart had bought ran out in the early hours of one August morning in 2001.

Mark Stewart, who had seen him in so much physical distress, says very quietly: 'I like to think he is comfortable now.'

NOTES:
[1] The BRDC tower, replacing the old single-storey building, is a sophisticated setting from which to watch races.
[2] Jungle juice: the fuel manfacturers prepared special fuels for their customers and they smelt . . . horrible. Someone once observed they were so potent that if there was ever a major fire in the pit lane the whole lot would go up and take the whole of Formula 1 with it.
[3] Michael Taylor, a Briton, had raced sports cars with success since 1958.

FAREWELL

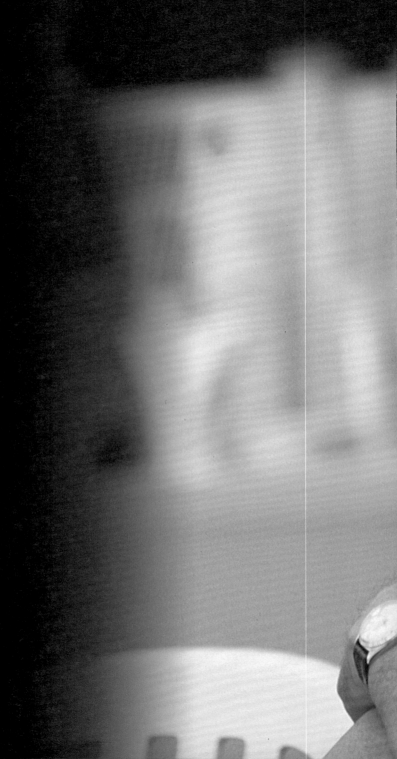

'He used to leave home in the dark at about 5.30 in the morning and, weather permitting, he arrived in Derbyshire in time to call at his favourite Little Chef roadside café near Matlock to have a full cooked English breakfast, chatting to the local lorry drivers.'

Paul Tear

'I asked him once if he believed in God, and I found his answer to be the best I've ever heard. "I'm not sure about God, but I do believe in the Ten Commandments and if you follow those you won't go far wrong."'

Julian Bailey

The Cathedral Church of the Holy Spirit stands alone on raised ground above Guildford, a long, tall, modern building but holding the timeless dignity of any cathedral. Those who remembered, those who came in through the big door looked, mostly, touched by the years. Ken's career had been a long one and whenever it – and he – began to touch you was probably a long time ago.

Those who remembered, those who came into the timeless dignity moved quietly to their seats – these people whose exploits had once made the earth tremble: Stewart and John Surtees, Alesi and Brundle, Palmer and Derek Bell and Bailey. Ron Dennis represented McLaren, Patrick Head represented Williams, Rob Walker represented the privateers who could still go motor racing when Ken's career got serious. Among the several hundred other people, all branches and aspects of motorsport were present and correct. Norah and Kenneth and Bob and the grandchildren

The old master never forgot the lesson he had learned that first day at Silverstone in 1951 – motor racing should give pleasure (Schlegelmilch).

came in together and travelled like a phalanx to their seats at the front – Norah already ill. She'd survived Ken by nine months. Grandson Adam would take the first Reading.

Before the memorial service – organised by the BRDC – the Band of the Royal Air Force Regiment played among others Elgar, Vaughan Williams, Holst, Debussy. The service was as these services are, a carefully constructed thing of favourite hymns and music with the Readings and Addresses threaded through.

I suppose, as we sat in the cathedral waiting for the service to begin, each of us moved gently back through memory. I remember the first time we spoke, Zandvoort in 1982, when he strode over: 'ah, you're the one doing it for the *Daily Express* now. I'll never forget when the *Express* had a big headline: 'FIRST 100MPH LAP AT SILVERSTONE' and nobody could believe it.' Then he strode away.

Honours aplenty and interviews always. Tyrrell is presented with the British Racing Drivers' Club Gold Medal in 1998 and talks to Murray Walker about it (Sutton).

I remember, *circa* 1984, the whole British press pack was on a flight to Paris for a day with Renault, and Tyrrell sat at the back of the plane looking mildly astonished to see the pack suddenly materialise. We assumed he was going to the FIA in the Place de la Concorde and he never said he wasn't. Only later did we realise he never said he was, either. He had been travelling, supposedly in great secrecy, to Renault to sign an engine deal – and did. From being suddenly cornered on a plane to outfoxing all of us gave him, I suspect, great joy and got somebody a froth job in the telling of it.

I remember our shared love of cricket (he once asked me to explain what bodyline bowling was), and how he delighted in the cricket stories he didn't know. Before one British Grand Prix, when he ought to have been supervising the team, I regaled him with the much-exaggerated legend surrounding a Somerset bowler called Bill Andrews, who greeted people by saying 'shake the hand that bowled Bradman'. Tyrrell listened intently, the motor racing far away from him now as I paraphrased what Andrews used to say.

'The all-conquering Australians are at Somerset and they're batting. I knew how to get Bloggs out and I did.

Australia 9 for 1 wicket. I knew how to get Jones, next, out and I did. Australia 12 for 2. In comes the great Don Bradman. I knew how to get him out and I did. Australia 394 for 3 . . .'

An American writer of motor racing fiction, Bob Judd, was sitting round the table and he exploded in laughter at this, while (of course) Tyrrell was frothing and guffawing.

I remember how he'd ring up during the 1984 fuel irregularity debacle and, behind that gruff exterior, it was hurting. The fact that Tyrrell was expunged from the records in 1984, making Bellof a non-person [in Soviet parlance] – and his epic drive at Monaco in the storm into something which did not happen – hurt, too. He believed that if the race had gone on long enough Bellof would have caught and overtaken Ayrton Senna. Brundle at Detroit had gone into the Gulag of the unremembered, too.

I remember how he smoked small cigars, my small cigars. He'd stride across and for such a big feller could look surprisingly humble. 'Just one,' he'd say. Then at a Tyrrell launch I opened the packet towards him but he said briskly 'stopped', and I don't think he ever smoked another. If he did, I didn't see him.

In the ranks of people in the cathedral, what memories were being relived in the privacy of silence? Hundreds, maybe thousands and, I bet, every one a good one: there had never been anything meagre about the big feller.

Paul Tear, his old shooting friend, gave the first Address and spoke of Tyrrell's ordinary approach to everything. Tear has kindly allowed me to reproduce extracts from the Address and I do so with gratitude because they capture aspects of Tyrrell which were not always on public view.

I first met Ken Tyrrell about 20 years ago when we were both members of the same shooting party, somewhere up in Leicestershire. Subsequently and almost without a break we met regularly at least a couple of times a week throughout the winter months and spent many happy hours together in each other's company, sharing our mutual love of the countryside and shooting.

Just over two years ago a very dear friend of mine, and a good pal of Ken's, died in his early 60s. Being a close friend of the family I had been asked to say a few words

about our mutual friend at his memorial service. Ken travelled up to Sheffield for the service and afterwards I gave him a lift to a local hostelry, where family and friends were gathering.

On the way to the hotel Ken was kind enough to compliment me on my performance and asked me to promise that I would so something similar for him one day. I must say I thought he was being jocular at the time but I agreed nevertheless. I didn't realise that Ken's request was so specific – because I subsequently learned that only two or three days beforehand he had been diagnosed as having cancer, and it was only then that I realised how poignant his request was.

His son Kenneth tells me that shortly before he died, Ken recounted this story to him and asked him to get me to keep my promise, so here I am. Ken's love of the countryside and shooting must surely emanate from the days of his youth when, as a boy, he accompanied his gamekeeper father on shoots, picking up spent cartridge cases and generally fetching and carrying for the team of guns. Apart from enjoying his day the half-a-crown-a-day wages impressed Ken most. So: Ken the careful.

[After the war ended] Ken and his crew were flying Lancasters of Transport Command with supplies out to our forces in India and the Far East. To augment the RAF's meagre wages, Ken and his crew decided to help with the post-war restrictions by bringing home some of life's little luxuries, such as teas, and silks, and the odd carpet or two – a veritable modern competitor to the East India Company. So: Ken the entrepreneur.

The good times which will always live: Cevert at Monaco in 1972, giving it plenty (Schlegelmilch).

Ken was very English and hated losing. I remember once sitting in the stands at Twickenham with him, having watched England demolish the Scots at Rugby – I think 19-18, that sort of demolition! – and with that knowing, boyish grin he turned to me and said: "That was most satisfying. The only problem is Norah won't be very pleased."

He used to leave home in the dark at about 5.30 in the morning and, weather permitting, he arrived in Derbyshire in time to call at his favourite Little Chef roadside café near Matlock to have a full cooked English breakfast, chatting to the local lorry drivers, who knew him well – and helping to put the world right on any subject, before joining us for shooting.

Sadly, the Little Chef in Matlock is now an Indian take-away but after great perseverance, and the help of the Restaurant Group's Managing Director, I have been able to track down an award that was presented to Ken by the manageress of the Happy Eater a couple of years ago, in recognition of his patronage of their establishment over many years. Here it is.

Ken was greatly amused by this gift at the time, and you can just imagine him pontificating on a topic of the day with his trucker pals – [he] dressed in his plus-fours,

shooting kit, tie neatly around his neck eating sausage, fried egg and bacon rasher. The mind boggles, doesn't it?

After Tear, there was the hymn *Guide me, O thou great Redeemer* and the second Reading by Kenneth. Dame Kiri Te Kanawa sang *Morgen* by Richard Strauss, sang it without a microphone, sang it so that her voice seemed shaped like crystal, the sounds pure and glistening and cutting the stillness, immortally beautiful. Jackie Stewart talked as only he can, dancing between memory and insight and humour.

Then the Chris Barber Band played *The Panama Rag* and, when the prayers and hymns and the blessing were done, the Barber Band came up the aisle giving *When the Saints Go Marching In* a real belting, their movements rocking with the rhythm – heads dipping and rising, bodies bouncing. This was a cascading of sound and it was wonderfully, wonderfully alive, just as Ken Tyrrell had been.

Somebody said: 'Ken would have loved that', to which somebody else, clearly a believer, added: 'Ken did.'

The big feller, you see, left a big hole and it remains unfilled.

It always will.

The big feller, in his pomp (Phipps/Sutton).

KEN TYRRELL:
The personal racing record

I am completely indebted to Duncan Rabagliati for painstaking research in putting together Ken Tyrrell's career as a driver. I am also indebted to Martin Hadwen for adding details here and there – each valuable, if you care about these things. Because Tyrrell's driving career was modest in character the races tended to be minor ones on crowded programmes and in some cases the results are simply not known. I have included them for two reasons: to try to make the record as complete as possible; and to show how much driving Tyrrell did in how many places. This in turn helps you to understand how much practical knowledge and experience he had gathered when he moved into team management.

Between 1952 and 1956 he competed in Formula 3, which was 500cc. He seems to have had 1957 off!

DNF = Did Not Finish; NK = Not Known; DNS = Did Not Start; NC = Not Classified; FL = Fastest Lap; W = withdrawn.

THE DRIVER

1952

Goodwood, 2 June	Goodwood Int.	DNF
Boreham, 2 Aug	Boreham Int.	Reserve
Silverstone, 23 Aug	Cdr Yorke Trophy	
	Heat 2	10
	Final	DNF
Silverstone, 20 Sept	Peterborough M.C.	DNF (crash)
Brands Hatch, 21 Sept	Consolation race	NK
Castle Combe, 4 Oct	Heat 2	8
	Final	NK
Brands Hatch, 12 Oct	Heat 2	NK
	Consolation race	NK

1953

Goodwood, 6 Apr		DNF (crash)
Beveridge Park, 25 Apr	Race 1	
	Heat 3	1
	Final	2
	Race 2	
	Heat 4	1
	Final	1
Brands Hatch, 3 May	Heat 2	NK
Charterhall, 23 May		2
Thruxton, 25 May		DNF (spin, stall)
Snetterton, 30 May		5
Snetterton, 27 June		5
Snetterton, 11 July		1
Snetterton, 25 July		Front row of grid
		NK
Davidstow, 1 Aug	Heat 1	4
	Final	6
Thruxton, 3 Aug		DNS
Charterhall, 15 Aug		DNS
Silverstone, 22 Aug	Cdr Yorke Trophy	3
	100 miles	2
Goodwood, 26 Sept		NK
Oulton Park, 3 Oct	Heat 2	2
	Final	2
Snetterton, 17 Oct		NK

1954

Kirkistown, 20 Mar	Irish 500cc	3
Brands Hatch, 19 Apr	Heat 2	1
	Final	2
	Senior race	2
Brands Hatch, 1 May	Senior	NK
	Whitsun Invitation	NK
Ibsley, 8 May		DNF (engine)
Silverstone, 15 May	Daily Express	DNF
Aintree, 29 May	Aintree '200'	DNF
Goodwood, 7 June		3
Oulton Park, 12 June		NK
Crystal Palace, 19 June		NK
Brands Hatch, 4 July	Open: Heat 1	NK
	Senior	NK
Oulton Park, 10 July	Heat 2	NK
Fairwood, 24 July	Heat 1	FL/4
	Final	NK
Davidstow, 2 Aug		2
Silverstone, 14 Aug		1
Silverstone, 21 Aug	Cdr Yorke Trophy	
	Race 2	2
Silverstone, 11 Sept		NK
Brighton Speed Trial, 4 Sept	500cc	1 (record)
Crystal Palace, 18 Sept	Heat 3	2
	Final	9
Goodwood, 25 Sept	Race 1	NK
Aintree, 2 Oct		DNF
Brands Hatch, 3 Oct	Heat 3	4
	Final	NC
Brands Hatch, 26 Dec	Christmas Trophy	5

1955

Goodwood, 11 Apr		NK
Ibsley, 30 Apr		5
Brands Hatch, 1 May	Heat 1	4
	1st Final	6
Silverstone, 7 May	Daily Express	11
Brands Hatch, 29 May	Heat 3	3
	Sporting Rec. Trophy	6
Davidstow, 30 May		1
Brands Hatch, 12 June	Heat 2	1
	1st Final	4
Brands Hatch, 10 July	Heat 2	1
	Sporting Rec. Trophy	NK
Aintree, 16 July	Grand Prix	NK
Crystal Palace, 30 July		DNS
Brands Hatch, 1 Aug	Heat 3	5
	Daily Telegraph Trophy	NK
Råbelöv, 6 Aug	Swedish GP	DNF
Karlskoga, 14 Aug		1

Oulton Park, 27 Aug	Heat	NK
	Final	DNS (ignition)
Brands Hatch, 4 Sept	Heat 1	3
	Trophy	NK
Silverstone, 10 Aug	Race 1	1
	Race 2	2
Silverstone, 17 Sept	Cdr Yorke Trophy	
	Heat 1	3
	Final	7
Oulton Park, 24 Sept	Gold Cup	DNF (clutch)
Brands Hatch, 9 Oct	Heat 2	NK
Brands Hatch, 26 Dec	Heat 1	2
	Yuletide Trophy	5

1956

Goodwood, 2 Apr		6
Aintree '200,' 21 Apr		8
Brands Hatch, 29 Apr	Heat 2	3
	Final	NK
Silverstone, 5 May	Daily Express	7th in practice
Goodwood, 21 May	Goodwood	DNS

1958 (Formula 2)

Pau, 7 Apr	Grand Prix	DNF
Aintree '200,' 19 Apr		11
Brands Hatch, 18 May	Heat 1	4
	Heat 2	2
	Overall	4
Crystal Palace, 26 May	Heat 2	1
	Final	6
Brands Hatch, 4 Aug	Heat 1	9
	Heat 2	7
	Aggregate	7

THE TEAM MANAGER

1960 (Formula Junior)

Goodwood, 18 Mar	John Surtees	2
Oulton, 2 Apr	Surtees	DNF
	Henry Taylor	4
Goodwood, 18 Apr	Taylor	4
	Keith Ballisat	5
	Tom Dickson	7
Aintree '200,' 30 Apr	Taylor	2
	Surtees	DNF
Silverstone Int., 14 May	Surtees	2
	Taylor	DNF (clutch)
Monaco, 28 May	Taylor	1
Crystal Palace, 6 June	Taylor	DNS
	Ballisat	DNF (crash)
Albi, 12 June	Taylor	
	Heat 1	1
	Final	1/FL
	Ian Raby	
	Heat 2	1
	Final	2

Monza, 29 June	Raby	
	Heat 2	2
	Final	DNF (crash)
	Taylor Heat 2	DNF
Reims, 3 July	Ballisat Heat 2	5 (6th agg)
	Raby	
	Heat 1	6
	Heat 2	4 (4th agg)
Reims, 7 July	Ballisat	5
	Raby	4
Silverstone, 16 July	Denny Hulme	6
Brands Hatch, 17 July	Taylor	3
Solitude, 24 July	Taylor	DNF (engine)
	Ballisat	5
Brands Hatch, 1 Aug	Surtees	4
	Taylor	5
Pescara, 15 Aug	John Love	3
	Ballisat	6
Goodwood, 20 Aug	Love	8
	Surtees	DNS
Brands Hatch, 27 Aug	Surtees	3
	Taylor	DNS
Snetterton, 17 Sept	Surtees	4
	Taylor	7
Oulton Gold Cup, 24 Sept	Surtees	DNF (overheating)
	Taylor	6
	Ballisat	12
Silverstone, 1 Oct	Taylor	1
	Hulme	5
Brands Hatch, 26 Dec	Surtees	DNS
	Taylor	DNF (engine)

1961 (Formula Junior)

Cesenatico, 2 Apr	Love	6
Goodwood, 4 Apr	Tony Maggs	1
	Love	DNS
Oulton Park, 15 Apr	Maggs	14
	Love	2
Aintree, 22 Apr	Maggs	DNF (throttle linkage)
	Love	3
Silverstone, 5 May	Maggs	3
	Love	6
Monaco, 13 May	Love	2
	Maggs	3
Chimay, 21 May	Love	1
	Maggs	2
Brands Hatch, 3 June	Maggs	9
	Love	4
Rouen, 4 June	Maggs	1
	Love	2
Charterhall, 17 June	Maggs	2
La Châtre, 25 June	Love	1
	Maggs	DNF
Monza, 26 June	Maggs	1
	Love	NK

Reims, 2 July	Love	5 (agg)
	Maggs	2 (agg)
Silverstone, British Empire Trophy, 8 July	Love Race 1	5
	Maggs Race 2	2
Solitude, 23 July	Love	DNF (piston)
	Maggs	3
Brands Hatch, 7 Aug	Love	5
	Maggs	3
Nogaro, 13 Aug	Maggs	4
	Love	1
Karlskoga, 20 Aug	Maggs	1
	Love	2
Roskildering, 27 Aug	Maggs	2 (agg)
	Love	1 (agg)
Zandvoort, 3 Sept	Love	DNF (crash)
	Maggs	1
Oulton Gold Cup, 23 Sept	Maggs	1
	Love	3
Snetterton, 30 Sept	Love	7
	Maggs	3
Montlhéry, 8 Oct	Maggs	1 (agg)*
	Love	1 (agg)*

* They had exactly the same time!

1962 (Formula Junior)

Oulton, 7 Apr	Maggs	2
	Love	3
Snetterton, 14 Apr	Maggs	5
	Love	4
Goodwood, 23 Apr	Maggs	DNF (crash)
	Love	4
Aintree '200', 28 Apr	Maggs	2
	Love	3
Silverstone, 12 May	Love	8
	Maggs	2
Roskildering, 17 May	Love	1 (agg)
	Hulme	2 (agg)
Monaco, 2 June	Love	DNF
	Peter Proctor	NK
Magny-Cours, 3 June	Love	1
	José Rosinski	DNF (engine)
Mallory, 11 June	Maggs	5
La Châtre, 17 June	Love	NK
	Proctor	NK
Monza, 24 June	Maggs	5
	Love	6
Reims, 1 July	Maggs	5
	Love	DNF (crash)
	Hulme	4
Rouen, 8 July	Love	DNF (crash)
Charade, 15 July	Love	7 (agg)
	Maggs	1
Dunboyne, 28 July	Maggs	DNF (gearbox)
	Love	2
	Proctor	1
Brands Hatch, 6 Aug	Maggs	1

	Love	6
Karlskoga, 12 Aug	Maggs	2
	Love	1
Roskildering, 25/26 Sept	Maggs	2 (agg)
	Love	1 (agg)
Zandvoort, 2 Sept	Maggs	2
	Proctor	4
Albi, 9 Sept	Love	DNF (crash)
	Maggs	DNF (crash)
	Hulme	3
Snetterton, 29 Sept	Maggs	4
	Hulme	6

1963 (Formula Junior)

Goodwood, 5 Apr	Proctor	5
	John Rhodes	6
Aintree, 7 Apr	Rhodes	DNF (crash)
	Proctor	DNF (crash)
Silverstone, 11 May	Proctor	DNF (crash)
	Rhodes	8
Monaco, 25 May	Rosinski	DNS
	Proctor	4
Crystal Palace, 3 June	Chris Amon	DNF (lost wheel)
	Rhodes	8
Magny-Cours, 9 June	Rosinski	1 (agg)
Rouen, 23 June	Tim Mayer	7
	Rosinski	DNF
Reims, 30 June	Proctor	9
	Mayer	8
Clermont Ferrand, 7 July	Proctor	DNF
	Mayer	4 (agg)
Silverstone, 20 July	Proctor	DNF (crash)
	Mayer	DNF (crash)
Phoenix Park, 27 July	Proctor	4
	Mayer	DNS
Roskildering, 18 Aug	Mayer	3
	Proctor	4
Goodwood, 24 Aug	Mayer	DNF (engine)
	Mayer	DNF (crash)
Zolder, 25 Aug	Mayer	DNS
	Proctor	5
Albi, 8 Sept	Rhodes	10
	Mayer	DNS
Brands Hatch, 14 Sept	Mayer	6
	Peter Revson	DNF (crash)
Snetterton, 28 Sept	Mayer	4
	Amon	DNS

1964 (Formula 3)

Mallory, 6 Mar	John Taylor	1
Snetterton, 14 Mar	Jackie Stewart	1
Goodwood, 30 Mar	Warwick Banks	3
	Stewart	1
Oulton, 11 Apr	Stewart	1
	Banks	2
Aintree, 18 Apr	Stewart	1
	Banks	DNS
Silverstone, 2 May	Stewart	1

	Banks	2
Monza, 7 May	Banks	3
Monaco, 9 May	Stewart	1
Mallory, 17 May	Banks	2
	Stewart	1
La Châtre, 7 June	Stewart	2
	Banks	7
Rouen, 28 June	Stewart	1
	Banks	2
Reims, 4 July	Stewart	1
	Banks	DNF
Brands Hatch, 3 Aug	Stewart	6
	Banks	1
Zolder, 23 Aug	Stewart	DNS
Zandvoort, 30 Aug	Stewart	1
	Rhodes	4
Oulton, 19 Sept	Stewart	1
	Love	4
Snetterton, 26 Sept	Banks	DNS
Mallory, 11 Oct	Banks	DNF (crash)

1964 (Formula 2)

Karlskoga, 9 Aug	Stewart	DNS
	Banks	11

1965 (Formula 2)

Silverstone, 20 Mar	Frank Gardner	DNS (rain)
	Stewart	DNS
Oulton, 3 Apr	Stewart	2
	Gardner	DNS
Snetterton, 10 Apr	Stewart	DNF
Pau, 25 Apr	Stewart	5
	Gardner	DNF
Crystal Palace, 7 June	Stewart	DNF
	Surtees	DNF
Reims, 4 July	Surtees	DNF
	Stewart	5
Rouen, 11 July	Bob Bondurant	DNF
	Stewart	DNF
Karlskoga, 8 Aug	Stewart	DNF
Pergusa, 8 Aug	Amon	6
Oulton, 11 Sept	Stewart	NC
	Bondurant	DNF (crash)
Albi, 26 Sept	Bondurant	8
	Ludovico Scarfiotti	DNF (chassis)

1965 (Formula 3)

Silverstone, 20 Mar	Banks	1
Goodwood, 19 Apr	Banks	DNS
Pau, 25 Apr	Banks	DNS
Silverstone, 15 May	Banks	DNF
Monaco, 29 May	Bondurant	DNF (crash)
Silverstone, 10 July	Bondurant	8

1966 (Formula 2)

Oulton, 2 Apr	Stewart	DNS (snow!)
	Ickx	DNS
Goodwood, 11 Apr	Stewart	DNF

	Ickx	6
Pau, 17 Apr	Stewart	DNF
	Ickx	4
Barcelona, 24 Apr	Stewart	2
	Mike Spence	DNF (crash)
Zolder, 8 May	Ickx	NC
Reims, 3 July	Surtees	DNF (piston)
	Ickx	NC
Rouen, 10 July	Surtees	7
	Ickx	DNF
Nürburgring, 7 Aug	Hubert Hahne	2
	Ickx	DNF
Montlhéry, 11 Sept	Stewart	4
	Hahne	10
Le Mans, 18 Sept	Stewart	4
	Ickx	DNF
Albi, 25 Sept	Stewart	DNF (valve)
	Ickx	4
Brands Hatch, 30 Oct	Scarfiotti (Heat 1)	8
	Ickx	4

1967 (Formula 2)

Snetterton, 24 Mar	Stewart	DNF (fuel feed)
	Ickx	DNF
Silverstone, 27 Mar	Stewart	5 (agg)
	Ickx	7 (agg)
Pau, 2 Apr	Stewart	DNF (clutch)
	Ickx	5
Barcelona, 9 Apr	Stewart	DNF (brakes)
	Ickx	DNF (engine)
Oulton, 18 Apr	Ickx	W
Nürburgring, 23 Apr	Ickx	3
Mallory, 14 May	Ickx	1
Zolder, 21 May	Ickx	DNF (engine)
Crystal Palace, 29 May	Ickx	1
	Jean-Pierre Jaussaud	DNF (fuel feed)
Reims, 25 June	Stewart	4
	Ickx	6
Rouen, 9 July	Stewart	DNF (crash)
Hockenheim, 9 July	Ickx	10 (agg)
Vienna, 16 July	Ickx	5
Jarama, 23 July	Stewart	2
	Jaussaud	DNF (clutch)
Zandvoort, 30 July	Ickx	1
Nürburgring, 6 Aug	Ickx	NC
Karlskoga, 13 Aug	Stewart	1
	Ickx	6
Pergusa, 20 Aug	Ickx	3
	Stewart	1
Brands Hatch, 28 Aug	Stewart	2
	Ickx	5
Oulton, 16 Sept	Ickx	DNF (crash)
	Stewart	1
Albi, 24 Sept	Stewart	1
	Ickx	4
Vallelunga, 8 Oct	Ickx	1 (agg)
	Jaussaud	6

TYRRELL:
The complete Grand Prix record

Note: the drivers' points refer only to Tyrrell so that, for example, in 1989 Johnny Herbert scored 5 points for Benetton before driving one race for Tyrrell, where he did not score. His total appears as 0. Note also that if a driver wasn't running at the end but was classified, the position where he finished is given.

Although the Tyrrell team was not in contention for the Constructors' Championship from the late 1970s, and its drivers not in contention for the World Championship from about the same time, for direct comparison I give the first three in each season, by season with whatever Tyrrell did afterwards.

DNF = Did Not Finish; FL = Fastest Lap; P = Pole; DNS = Did Not Start; NC = Not Classified; DSQ = Disqualified; DNQ = Did Not Qualify; u.j. = universal joint.

1968 (Matra-Ford)

South Africa	Kyalami	J. Stewart	DNF (engine)
Spain	Jarama	J-P. Beltoise	5
Monaco	Monte Carlo	Servoz-Gavin	DNF (driveshaft)
Belgium	Spa	J. Stewart	4
Holland	Zandvoort	J. Stewart	1
France	Rouen	J. Stewart	3
Great Britain	Brands Hatch	J. Stewart	6
Germany	Nürburgring	J. Stewart	FL/1
Italy	Monza	J. Stewart	DNF (engine
		J. Servoz-Gavin	2
Canada	Mont-Tremblant	J. Stewart	6
		J. Servoz-Gavin	DNF (crash)
USA	Watkins Glen	J. Stewart	FL/1
Mexico	Mexico City	J. Stewart	7
		J. Servoz-Gavin	DNF (ignition)

Championship: G. Hill (Lotus) 48; Stewart 36; Denny Hulme (McLaren) 33; J. Servoz-Gavin 6 (13th). *Constructors':* Lotus 62; McLaren 49; Matra 45.

1969 (Matra-Ford)

South Africa	Kyalami	J. Stewart	FL/1
		J-P. Beltoise	6
Spain	Montjuich	J. Stewart	1
		J-P. Beltoise	3
Monaco	Monte Carlo	J. Stewart	P/FL/DNF (broken u.j.)
		J-P. Beltoise	DNF (broken u.j.)
Holland	Zandvoort	J. Stewart	FL/1
		J-P. Beltoise	8
France	Clermont-Ferrand	J. Stewart	P/FL/1
		J-P. Beltoise	2
Great Britain	Silverstone	J. Stewart	FL/1
		J-P. Beltoise	9
Germany	Nürburgring	J. Stewart	2
		J-P. Beltoise	12
Italy	Monza	J. Stewart	1
		J-P. Beltoise	FL/3

(Schlegelmilch)

Canada	Mosport	J. Stewart	DNF (crash)
		J-P. Beltoise	4
		J. Servoz-Gavin	6
USA	Watkins Glen	J. Stewart	DNF (engine)
		J-P. Beltoise	DNF (engine)
		J. Servoz-Gavin	NC
Mexico	Mexico City	J. Stewart	4
		J-P. Beltoise	5
		J. Servoz-Gavin	8

Championship: Stewart 63; J. Ickx (Brabham) 37; B. McLaren (McLaren) 26; Beltoise 21 (5th); Servoz-Gavin 1 (16th). *Constructors':* Matra 66; Brabham 51; Lotus 47.

1970 (March-Ford – Stewart last three races in Tyrrell-Ford)

South Africa	Kyalami	J. Stewart	P/3
		Servoz-Gavin	DNF (engine)
Spain	Jarama	J. Stewart	1
		J. Servoz-Gavin	5
Monaco	Monte Carlo	J. Servoz-Gavin	DNS
		J. Stewart	P/DNF (engine)
Belgium	Spa	J. Stewart	P/DNF (engine)
Holland	Zandvoort	J. Stewart	2
		F. Cevert	DNF (engine)
France	Clermont-Ferrand	J. Stewart	9
		F. Cevert	11
Great Britain	Brands Hatch	J. Stewart	DNF (fire)
		F. Cevert	7
Germany	Hockenheim	J.Stewart	DNF (engine)
		F. Cevert	7
Austria	Österreichring	J. Stewart	DNF (split fuel line)
		F. Cevert	DNF (engine)

Italy	Monza	J. Stewart	2
		F. Cevert	6
Canada	Mont-Tremblant	F. Cevert	9
		J. Stewart	P/ DNF (stub axle)
USA	Watkins Glen	J. Stewart	DNF (oil leak)
		F. Cevert	DNF (lost wheel)
Mexico	Mexico City	J. Stewart	DNF (suspension)
		F. Cevert	DNF (engine)

Championship: J. Rindt (Lotus) 45; J. Ickx (Ferrari) 40; C. Regazzoni (Ferrari) 33; Stewart 25 (5th); Servoz-Gavin 2 (19th); Cevert 1 (22nd). *Constructors':* Lotus 59; Ferrari 55; March 48; Matra 23 (6th.)

1971 (Tyrrell-Ford)

South Africa	Kyalami	J. Stewart	P/2
		F. Cevert	DNF (accident)
Spain	Montjuich	J. Stewart	1
		F. Cevert	7
Monaco	Monte Carlo	J. Stewart	P/FL/1
		F. Cevert	DNF (suspension & crash)
Holland	Zandvoort	J. Stewart	11
		F. Cevert	DNF (crash)
France	Ricard	J. Stewart	P/FL/1
		F. Cevert	2
Great Britain	Silverstone	J. Stewart	FL/1
		F. Cevert	10
Germany	Nürburgring	J. Stewart	P/1
		F. Cevert	FL/2
Austria	Österreichring	J. Stewart	DNF (driveshaft, wheel)
		F. Cevert	DNF (engine)
Italy	Monza	F. Cevert	3
		J. Stewart	DNF (engine)
Canada	Mosport	J. Stewart	P/1
		F. Cevert	6
USA	Watkins Glen	J. Stewart	P/5
		F. Cevert	1
		P. Revson	DNF (clutch)

Championship: Stewart 62; R. Peterson (March) 33; Cevert 26. *Constructors':* Tyrrell 73; BRM 36; March 33.

1972 (Tyrrell-Ford)

Argentina	Buenos Aires	J. Stewart	FL/1
		F. Cevert	DNF (gearbox)
South Africa	Kyalami	J. Stewart	P/DNF (gearbox)
		F. Cevert	9
Spain	Jarama	J. Stewart	DNF (crash)
		F. Cevert	DNF (engine)
Monaco	Monte Carlo	J. Stewart	4
		F. Cevert	NC
Belgium	Nivelles	F. Cevert	2
France	Clermont-Ferrand	J. Stewart	1
		F. Cevert	4
		P. Depailler	NC
Great Britain	Brands Hatch	J. Stewart	FL/2
		F. Cevert	DNF (crash)

Germany	Nürburgring	J. Stewart	11
		F. Cevert	10
Austria	Österreichring	J. Stewart	7
		F. Cevert	9
Italy	Monza	J. Stewart	DNF (clutch)
		F. Cevert	DNF (engine)
Canada	Mosport	J. Stewart	FL/1
		F. Cevert	DNF (gearbox)
USA	Watkins Glen	J. Stewart	P/FL/1
		F. Cevert	2
		P. Depailler	7

Championship: E, Fittipaldi (Lotus) 61; Stewart 45; Hulme (McLaren) 39; Cevert 15 (6th); Depailler 0. *Constructors':* Lotus 61; Tyrrell 51; McLaren 47.

1973 (Tyrrell-Ford)

Argentina	Buenos Aires	J. Stewart	3
		F. Cevert	2
Brazil	Interlagos	J. Stewart	2
		F. Cevert	10
South Africa	Kyalami	J. Stewart	1
		F. Cevert	NC
Spain	Montjuich	J. Stewart	DNF (brakes)
		F. Cevert	2
Belgium	Zolder	J. Stewart	1
		F. Cevert	FL/2
Monaco	Monte Carlo	J. Stewart	P/1
		F. Cevert	4
Sweden	Anderstorp	J. Stewart	5
		F. Cevert	3
France	Ricard	J. Stewart	P/4
		F. Cevert	2
Great Britain	Silverstone	J. Stewart	10
		F. Cevert	5
Holland	Zandvoort	J. Stewart	1
		F. Cevert	2

(Schlegelmilch)

Germany	Nürburgring	J. Stewart	P/1
		F. Cevert	2
Austria	Österreichring	J. Stewart	2
		F. Cevert	DNF (crash)
Italy	Monza	J. Stewart	FL/4
		F. Cevert	5
Canada	Mosport	J. Stewart	5
		F. Cevert	DNF (crash)
		C. Amon	l0
USA	Watkins Glen	J. Stewart	DNS
		F. Cevert	(fatal crash, practice)
		C. Amon	DNS

Championship: Stewart 71; Fittipaldi (Lotus) 55; Peterson (Lotus) 52; F. Cevert 47 (4th); Amon 0. ***Constructors':*** Lotus 92; Tyrrell 82; McLaren 58 pts.

1974 (Tyrrell-Ford)

Argentina	Buenos Aires	J. Scheckter	DNF (cylinder head gasket)
		P. Depailler	6
Brazil	Interlagos	J. Scheckter	l3
		P. Depailler	8
South Africa	Kyalami	J. Scheckter	8
		P. Depailler	4
Spain	Jarama	J. Scheckter	5
		P. Depailler	8
Belgium	Nivelles	J. Scheckter	3
		P. Depailler	DNF (brakes)
Monaco	Monte Carlo	J. Scheckter	2
		P. Depailler	9
Sweden	Anderstorp	J. Scheckter	1
		P. Depailler	P/FL/2
Holland	Zandvoort	J. Scheckter	5
		P. Depailler	6
France	Dijon-Prenois	J. Scheckter	FL/4
		P. Depailler	8
Great Britain	Brands Hatch	J. Scheckter	1
		P. Depailler	DNF (engine)
Germany	Nürburgring	J. Scheckter	FL/2
		P. Depailler	DNF (crash damage)
Austria	Österreichring	J. Scheckter	DNF (engine)
		P. Depailler	DNF (crash)
Italy	Monza	J. Scheckter	3
		P. Depailler	11
Canada	Mosport	J. Scheckter	DNF (crash)
		P. Depailler	5
USA	Watkins Glen	J. Scheckter	DNF (fuel pipe)
		P. Depailler	6

Championship: Fittipaldi (McLaren) 55; Regazzoni (Ferrari); 52, Scheckter 45; Depailler 14 (9th). ***Constructors':*** McLaren 73; Ferrari 65; Tyrrell 52.

1975 (Tyrrell-Ford)

Argentina	Buenos Aires	J. Scheckter	11
		P Depailler	5
Brazil	Interlagos	J. Scheckter	DNF (split oil tank)
		P. Depailler	DNF (crash)

South Africa	Kyalami	J. Scheckter	1
		P. Depailler	3
Spain	Montjuich	J. Scheckter	DNF (engine)
		P. Depailler	DNF (crash)
Monaco	Monte Carlo	J. Scheckter	7
		P. Depailler	FL/5
Belgium	Zolder	J. Scheckter	2
		P. Depailler	4
Sweden	Anderstorp	J. Scheckter	7
		P. Depailler	l2
Holland	Zandvoort	J. Scheckter	16
		P. Depailler	9
France	Ricard	J. Scheckter	9
		P. Depailler	6
		J-P. Jabouille	l2
Great Britain	Silverstone	J. Scheckter	3
		P. Depailler	9
Germany	Nürburgring	J. Scheckter	DNF (crash)
		P. Depailler	9
Austria	Österreichring	J. Scheckter	8
		P. Depailler	11
Italy	Monza	J. Scheckter	8
		P. Depailler	7
USA	Watkins Glen	J. Scheckter	6
		P. Depailler	DNF (crash)
		M. Leclère	DNF (engine)

Championship: N. Lauda (Ferrari) 64.5; Fittipaldi (McLaren) 45; C. Reutemann (Brabham) 37; Scheckter 20 (7th); Depailler 12 (9th); Leclère 0. ***Constructors':*** Ferrari 72.5; Brabham 54; McLaren 53; Tyrrell 25 (5th).

1976 (Tyrrell-Ford)

Brazil	Interlagos	J. Scheckter	5
		P. Depailler	2
South Africa	Kyalami	J. Scheckter	4
		P. Depailler	9
USA West	Long Beach	J. Scheckter	DNF (suspension)
		P. Depailler	3
Spain	Jarama	J. Scheckter	DNF (engine, oil pump belt)
		P. Depailler	DNF (crash)
Belgium	Zolder	J. Scheckter	4
		P. Depailler	DNF (engine)
Monaco	Monte Carlo	J. Scheckter	2
		P. Depailler	3
Sweden	Anderstorp	J. Scheckter	P/1
		P. Depailler	2
France	Ricard	J. Scheckter	6
		P. Depailler	2
Great Britain	Brands Hatch	J. Scheckter	2
		P. Depailler	DNF (engine)
Germany	Nürburgring	J. Scheckter	FL/2
		P. Depailler	DNF (crash)
Austria	Österreichring	J. Scheckter	DNF (crash)
		P. Depailler	DNF (suspension breakage)

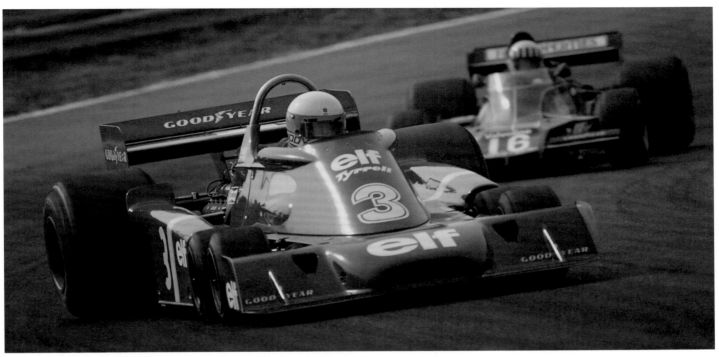

The six-wheeler in Holland, 1976, where Jody Scheckter finished fifth. (Schlegelmilch)

Holland	Zandoort	J. Scheckter	5
		P. Depailler	7
Italy	Monza	J. Scheckter	5
		P. Depailler	6
Canada	Mosport	J. Scheckter	4
		P. Depailler	FL/2
USA East	Watkins Glen	J. Scheckter	2
		P. Depailler	DNF (fuel line detached)
Japan	Mount Fuji	J. Scheckter	DNF (engine, overheating)
		P. Depailler	2

Championship: J. Hunt (McLaren) 69; Lauda (Ferrari) 68; Scheckter 49; Depailler 39 (4th). **Constructors':** Ferrari 83; McLaren 74; Tyrrell 71. Note: Three drivers entered Tyrrells privately. Alessandro Pesenti-Rossi, an Italian, drove in Germany, Austria, Holland (DNQ) and Italy. Otto Stuppacher, an Austrian, DNS in Italy, DNQ in Canada and the USA East. Kazuyoshi Hoshino, a Japanese, drove in Japan but retired. None scored a point.

1977 (Tyrrell-Ford)

Argentina	Buenos Aires	R. Peterson	DNF (spin)
		P. Depailler	DNF (engine overheating)
Brazil	Interlagos	R. Peterson	DNF (crash)
		P. Depailler	DNF (crash)
South Africa	Kyalami	R. Peterson	DNF (fuel pressure)
		P. Depailler	3
USA West	Long Beach	R. Peterson	DNF (fuel line)
		P. Depailler	4
Spain	Jarama	R. Peterson	8
		P. Depailler	DNF (engine)
Monaco	Monte Carlo	R. Peterson	DNF (brakes)
		P. Depailler	DNF (brakes, gearbox)
Belgium	Zolder	R. Peterson	3
		P. Depailler	8
Sweden	Anderstorp	R. Peterson	DNF (ignition)
		P. Depailler	4
France	Dijon-Prenois	R. Peterson	12
		P. Depailler	DNF (crash)
Great Britain	Silverstone	R. Peterson	DNF (engine)
		P. Depailler	DNF (crash)
Germany	Hockenheim	R. Peterson	9
		P. Depailler	DNF (engine)
Austria	Österreichring	R. Peterson	5
		P. Depailler	13
Holland	Zandvoort	R. Peterson	DNF (ignition)
		P. Depailler	DNF (engine)
Italy	Monza	R. Peterson	6
		P. Depailler	DNF (engine)

USA East	Watkins Glen	R. Peterson	l6
		P. Depailler	l4
Canada	Mosport	R. Peterson	DNF (fuel leak)
		P. Depailler	2
Japan	Mount Fuji	R. Peterson	DNF (crash)
		P. Depailler	3

Championship: Lauda (Ferrari) 72; Scheckter (Wolf) 55; M. Andretti (Lotus) 47; Depailler 20 (8th); Peterson 7 (14th) *Constructors':* Ferrari 95; Lotus 62; McLaren 60; Tyrrell 27 (5th).
Note: Kunimitsu Takahashi, a Japanese, in a privately entered Tyrrell (the one Hoshino had entered the year before!) finished ninth in Japan.

1978 (Tyrrell-Ford)

Argentina	Buenos Aires	D. Pironi	l4
		P. Depailler	3
Brazil	Jacarepagua	D. Pironi	6
		P. Depailler	DNF (brakes)
South Africa	Kyalami	D. Pironi	6
		P. Depailler	2
USA West	Long Beach	D. Pironi	DNF (gearbox)
		P. Depailler	3
Monaco	Monte Carlo	D. Pironi	5
		P. Depailler	1
Belgium	Zolder	D. Pironi	6
		P. Depailler	DNF (gearbox)
Spanish	Jarama	D. Pironi	l2
		P. Depailler	DNF (engine)
Sweden	Anderstorp	D. Pironi	DNF (puncture, suspension)
		P. Depailler	DNF (suspension)
France	Ricard	D. Pironi	10
		P. Depailler	DNF (engine)
Great Britain	Brands Hatch	D. Pironi	DNF (engine mounting bolts)
		Depailler	4
Germany	Hockenheim	D. Pironi	5
		P. Depailler	DNF (start line crash)
Austria	Österreichring	D. Pironi	DNF (crash)
		P. Depailler	2
Holland	Zandvoort	D. Pironi	DNF (crash)
		P. Depailler	DNF (engine)
Italy	Monza	D. Pironi	DNF (start line crash)
		P. Depailler	11
USA East	Watkins Glen	D. Pironi	10
		P. Depailler	DNF (loose hub)
Canada	Montreal	D. Pironi	7
		P. Depailler	5

Championship: Andretti (Lotus) 64; Peterson (Lotus) 51; Reutemann (Ferrari) 48; Depailler 34 (5th); Pironi 7 (15th). *Constructors':* Lotus 86; Ferrari 58; Brabham 53; Tyrrell 38 (4th).

1979 (Tyrrell-Ford)

Argentina	Buenos Aires	D. Pironi	DNF (start line crash)
		J-P. Jarier	DNF (engine)
Brazil	Interlagos	D. Pironi	4
		J-P. Jarier	DNS
South Africa	Kyalami	D. Pironi	DNF (throttle linkage)
		J-P. Jarier	3
USA West	Long Beach	D. Pironi	DSQ
		J-P. Jarier	6
Spain	Jarama	D. Pironi	6
		J-P. Jarier	5
Belgium	Zolder	D. Pironi	3
		J-P. Jarier	11
Monaco	Monte Carlo	D. Pironi	DNF (crash)
		J-P. Jarier	DNF (rear suspension)
France	Dijon-Prenois	D. Pironi	DNF (suspension)
		J-P. Jarier	5
Great Britain	Silverstone	D. Pironi	10
		J-P. Jarier	3
Germany	Hockenheim	D. Pironi	9
		G. Lees	7
Austria	Österreichring	D. Pironi	7
		D. Daly	8
Holland	Zandvoort	D. Pironi	DNF (rear suspension)
		J-P. Jarier	DNF (spin)
Italy	Monza	D. Pironi	l0
		J-P. Jarier	6
Canada	Montreal	D. Pironi	5
		J-P. Jarier	DNF (engine)
		D. Daly	DNF (engine)
USA East	Watkins Glen	D. Pironi	3
		J-P. Jarier	DNF (crash)
		D. Daly	DNF (crash)

Championship: Scheckter (Ferrari) 51; G. Villeneuve (Ferrari) 47; A. Jones (Williams) 40; Pironi 14, Jarier 14 (10th); Lees 0; Daly 0.
Constructors': Ferrari 113; Williams 75; Ligier 61; Tyrrell 28 (5th).

1980 (Tyrrell-Ford)

Argentina	Buenos Aires	J-P. Jarier	DNF (crash damage)
		D. Daly	4
Brazil	Interlagos	J-P. Jarier	l2
		D. Daly	l4
South Africa	Kyalami	J-P. Jarier	7
		D. Daly	DNF (puncture)
USA West	Long Beach	J-P. Jarier	DNF (crash)
		D. Daly	8
Belgium	Zolder	J-P. Jarier	5
		D. Daly	9
Monaco	Monte Carlo	J-P. Jarier	DNF (crash)
		D. Daly	DNF (crash)
Spain*	Jarama	J-P. Jarier	4
		D. Daly	DNF (crash)
France	Ricard	J-P. Jarier	l4
		D. Daly	11
Great Britain	Brands Hatch	J-P Jarier	5
		D. Daly	4
Germany	Hockenheim	J-P. Jarier	15
		D. Daly	10
Austria	Österreichring	J-P. Jarier	DNF (engine)
		D. Daly	DNF (crash)
Holland	Zandvoort	J-P. Jarier	5
		D. Daly	DNF (crash)

Italy	Imola	J-P. Jarier	DNF (brakes)
		D. Daly	DNF (crash)
Canada	Montreal	J-P. Jarier	7
		D. Daly	DNF (start line crash)
		M. Thackwell	DNF (car given to Jarier)
USA East	Watkins Glen	J-P. Jarier	NC
		D. Daly	DNF (suspension)
		M. Thackwell	DNQ

* non-championship

Championship: Jones (Williams) 67; N. Piquet (Brabham) 54; Reutemann (Williams) 42; Daly 6; Jarier 6 (10th); Thackwell 0.
Constructors': Williams 120; Ligier 66; Brabham 55; Tyrrell 12 (6th).

1981 (Tyrrell-Ford)

South Africa*	Kyalami	E. Cheever	7
		D. Wilson	DNF (crash)
USA West	Long Beach	E. Cheever	5
		K. Cogan	DNQ
Brazil	Jacarepagua	E. Cheever	NC
		R. Zunino	13
Argentina	Buenos Aires	E. Cheever	DNF (clutch)
		R. Zunino	13
San Marino	Imola	E. Cheever	DNF (crash)
		M. Alboreto	DNF (crash)
Belgium	Zolder	E. Cheever	6
		M. Alboreto	12
Monaco	Monte Carlo	E. Cheever	5
		M. Alboreto	DNF (crash)
Spain	Jarama	E. Cheever	NC
		M. Alboreto	DNQ
France	Dijon-Prenois	E. Cheever	13
		M. Alboreto	16
Great Britain	Silverstone	E. Cheever	4
		M. Alboreto	DNF (clutch)
Germany	Hockenheim	E. Cheever	5
		M. Alboreto	DNQ
Austria	Österreichring	E. Cheever	DNQ
		M. Alboreto	DNF (engine)
Holland	Zandvoort	E. Cheever	DNF (suspension)
		M. Alboreto	9
Italy	Monza	E. Cheever	DNF (crash)
		M. Alboreto	DNF (crash)
Canada	Montreal	E. Cheever	DNF (engine)
		M. Alboreto	11
USA	Las Vegas	E. Cheever	DNF (engine)
		M. Alboreto	DNF (engine)

* non-championship

Championship: Piquet (Brabham) 50; Reutemann (Williams) 49; Jones (Williams) 46; Cheever 10 (11th); Alboreto 0; Wilson 0; Cogan 0; Zunino 0.
Constructors': Williams 95; Brabham 61; Renault 54; Tyrrell 10 (8th).

(LAT)

1982 (Tyrrell-Ford)

South Africa	Kyalami	M. Alboreto	7
		S. Borgudd	16
Brazil	Jacarepagua	M. Alboreto	4
		S. Borgudd	7
USA West	Long Beach	M. Alboreto	4
		S. Borgudd	10
San Marino	Imola	M. Alboreto	3
		B. Henton	DNF (clutch)
Belgium	Zolder	M. Alboreto	DNF (engine)
		B. Henton	DNF (engine)
Monaco	Monte Carlo	M. Alboreto	10
		B. Henton	8
USA East	Detroit	M. Alboreto	DNF (crash)
		B. Henton	9
Canada	Montreal	M. Alboreto	DNF (gearbox)
		B. Henton	NC
Holland	Zandvoort	M. Alboreto	7
		B. Henton	DNF (throttle cable)
Great Britain	Brands Hatch	M. Alboreto	DNF (handling)
		B. Henton	FL/8
France	Ricard	M. Alboreto	6
		B. Henton	10
Germany	Hockenheim	M. Alboreto	4
		B. Henton	7
Austria	Österreichring	M. Alboreto	DNF (crash)
		B. Henton	DNF (engine)
Switzerland	Dijon-Prenois	M. Alboreto	7
		B. Henton	11
Italy	Monza	M. Alboreto	5
		B. Henton	DNF (crash)
USA	Las Vegas	M. Alboreto	FL/1
		B. Henton	8

Championship: K. Rosberg (Williams) 44; D. Pironi (Ferrari) and J. Watson (McLaren) 39; Alboreto 25 (7th); Henton 0; Borgudd 0.
Constructors': Ferrari 74; McLaren 69; Renault 62; Tyrrell 25 (6th).

1983 (Tyrrell-Ford)

Brazil	Jacerapagua	M. Alboreto	DNF (crash)
		D. Sullivan	11
USA West	Long Beach	M. Alboreto	9
		D. Sullivan	8
France	Ricard	M. Alboreto	8
		D. Sullivan	DNF (clutch)
San Marino	Imola	M. Alboreto	DNF (crash/ suspension)
		D. Sullivan	DNF (crash)
Monaco	Monte Carlo	M. Alboreto	DNF (crash)
		D. Sullivan	5
Belgium	Spa	M. Alboreto	14
		D. Sullivan	12
USA East	Detroit	M. Alboreto	1
		D. Sullivan	DNF (electrics)
Canada	Montreal	M. Alboreto	8
		D. Sullivan	DSQ
Great Britain	Silverstone	M. Alboreto	13
		D. Sullivan	14
Germany	Hockenheim	M. Alboreto	DNF (fuel pump)
		D. Sullivan	12
Austria	Österreichring	M. Alboreto	DNF (crash)
		D. Sullivan	DNF (crash)
Holland	Zandvoort	M. Alboreto	6
		D. Sullivan	DNF (engine)
Italy	Monza	M. Alboreto	DNF (clutch)
		D. Sullivan	DNF (fuel pump)
Europe	Brands Hatch	M. Alboreto	DNF (engine)
		D. Sullivan	DNF (fire)
South Africa	Kyalami	M. Alboreto	DNF (engine)
		D. Sullivan	7

Championship: Piquet (Brabham) 59; A. Prost (Renault) 57; R. Arnoux (Ferrari) 49; Alboreto 10 (12th); Sullivan 2 (17th).
Constructors': Ferrari 89; Renault 79; Brabham 72; Tyrrell 12 (7th).

1984 (Tyrrell-Ford)

Brazil	Jacarepagua	M. Brundle	5
		S. Bellof	DNF (throttle cable)
South Africa	Kyalami	M. Brundle	11
		S. Bellof	DNF (broken hub)
Belgium	Zolder	M. Brundle	DNF (lost wheel)
		S. Bellof	6
San Marino	Imola	M. Brundle	10
		S. Bellof	5
France	Dijon-Prenois	M. Brundle	12
		S. Bellof	DNF (gearbox)
Monaco	Monte Carlo	M. Brundle	DNQ
		S. Bellof	3
Canada	Montreal	M. Brundle	9
		S. Bellof	DNF (driveshaft)
USA East	Detroit	M. Brundle	2
		S. Bellof	DNF (crash)
USA	Dallas	M. Brundle	DNQ
		S. Bellof	DNF (hit wall)
Great Britain	Brands Hatch	S. Johansson	DNF (accident damage)
		S. Bellof	11
Germany	Hockenheim	S. Johansson	9
		M. Thackwell	DNQ
Austria	Österreichring	S. Johansson	DNQ
		S. Bellof	DNQ/DSQ*
Holland	Zandvoort	S. Johansson	8
		S. Bellof	9

* Car found to be under minimum weight in qualifying.
Note: Tyrrell were removed from the 1984 Championship because of a fuel irregularity, and each driver's points annulled. The team was banned from taking part in any of the Grands Prix after Holland.

1985 (Tyrrell-Ford)

Note: Renault engines from French GP

Brazil	Jacarepagua	M. Brundle	8
		S. Johansson	7
Portugal	Estoril	M. Brundle	DNF (gear linkage)
		S. Bellof	6
San Marino	Imola	M. Brundle	9
		S. Bellof	DNF (engine)
Monaco	Monte Carlo	M. Brundle	10
		S. Bellof	DNQ
Canada	Montreal	M. Brundle	12
		S. Bellof	11
USA East	Detroit	M. Brundle	DNF (crash)
		S. Bellof	4
France	Ricard	M. Brundle	DNF (gearbox)
		S. Bellof	13
Great Britain	Silverstone	M. Brundle	7
		S. Bellof	11
Germany	Nürburgring	M. Brundle	10
		S. Bellof	8
Austria	Österreichring	M. Brundle	DNQ
		S. Bellof	7
Holland	Zandvoort	M. Brundle	7
		S. Bellof	DNF (engine)
Italy	Monza	M. Brundle	8
Belgium	Spa	M. Brundle	13
Europe	Brands Hatch	M. Brundle	DNF (water pipe)
		I. Capelli	DNF (crash)
South Africa	Kyalami	M. Brundle	7
		P. Streiff	DNF (crash)
Australia	Adelaide	M. Brundle	NC
		I. Capelli	4

Championship: A. Prost (McLaren) 73; M. Alboreto (Ferrari) 53; Rosberg (Williams) 40; Bellof 4 (15th); Capelli 3 (17th); Brundle 0; Johnasson 0; Streiff 0. *Constructors':* McLaren 90; Ferrari 82; Williams and Lotus 71; Tyrrell 7 (9th).

1986 (Tyrrell-Renault)

Brazil	Jacarepagua	M. Brundle	5
		P. Streiff	7
Spain	Jerez	M. Brundle	DNF (oil loss)
		Streiff	DNF (oil loss)
San Marino	Imola	M. Brundle	8
		P. Streiff	DNF (transmission)

Monaco	Monte Carlo	M. Brundle	DNF (crash)
		P. Streiff	11
Belgium	Spa	M. Brundle	DNF (gearbox)
		P. Streiff	12
Canada	Montreal	M. Brundle	9
		P. Streiff	11
USA East	Detroit	M. Brundle	DNF (electrics)
		P. Streiff	9
France	Ricard	M. Brundle	10
		P. Streiff	DNF (fuel leak)
Great Britain	Brands Hatch	M. Brundle	5
		P. Streiff	6
Germany	Hockenheim	M. Brundle	DNF (electrics)
		P. Streiff	DNF (engine)
Hungary	Hungaroring	M. Brundle	6
		P. Streiff	8
Austria	Österreichring	M. Brundle	DNF (turbo)
		P. Streiff	DNF (engine)
Italy	Monza	M. Brundle	10
		P. Streiff	9
Portugal	Estoril	M. Brundle	DNF (engine)
		P. Streiff	DNF (engine)
Mexico	Mexico City	M. Brundle	11
		P. Streiff	DNF (turbo)
Australia	Adelaide	M. Brundle	4
		P. Streiff	5

Championship: Prost (McLaren) 72; N. Mansell (Williams) 70;
Piquet (Williams) 69; Brundle 8 (11th); Streiff 3 (13th).
Constructors': Williams l4l; Mclaren 96; Lotus 58; Tyrrell 11 (7th).

1987 (Tyrrell-Ford)

Brazil	Jacarepagua	J. Palmer	10
		P. Streiff	11
San Marino	Imola	J. Palmer	DNF (clutch)
		P. Streiff	8
Belgium	Spa	J. Palmer	DNF crash
		P. Streiff	9
Monaco	Monte Carlo	J. Palmer	5
		P. Streiff	DNF (crash)
USA East	Detroit	J. Palmer	11
		P. Streiff	DNF (crash)
France	Ricard	J. Palmer	7
		P. Streiff	6
Great Britain	Silverstone	J. Palmer	8
		P. Streiff	DNF (engine)
Germany	Hockenheim	J. Palmer	5
		P. Streiff	4
Hungary	Hungaroring	J. Palmer	7
		P. Streiff	9
Austria	Österreichring	J. Palmer	14
		P. Streiff	DNF (crash)
Italy	Monza	J. Palmer	14
		P. Streiff	12
Portugal	Estoril	J. Palmer	10
		P. Streiff	12
Spain	Jerez	J. Palmer	DNF (crash)
		P. Streiff	7

Mexico	Mexico City	J. Palmer	7
		P. Streiff	8
Japan	Suzuka	J. Palmer	8
		P. Streiff	12
Australia	Adelaide	J. Palmer	4
		P. Streiff	DNF (spin)

Championship: Piquet (Williams) 73; Mansell (Williams) 61;
A. Senna (Lotus) 57; Palmer 7 (11th); Streiff 4 (14th).
Constructors': Williams 137; McLaren 76; Lotus 64; Tyrrell 11 (6th).

1988 (Tyrrell-Ford)

Brazil	Jacarepagua	J. Palmer	DNF (transmission)
		J. Bailey	DNQ
San Marino	Imola	J. Palmer	14
		J. Bailey	DNF (gearbox)
Monaco	Monte Carlo	J. Palmer	5
		J. Bailey	DNQ
Mexico	Mexico City	J. Palmer	DNQ
		J. Bailey	DNQ
Canada	Montreal	J. Palmer	6
		J. Bailey	DNF (crash)
USA East	Detroit	J. Palmer	5
		J. Bailey	9
France	Ricard	J. Palmer	DNF (engine)
		J. Bailey	DNQ
Great Britain	Silverstone	J. Palmer	DNF (transmission)
		J. Bailey	16
Germany	Hockenheim	J. Palmer	11
		J. Bailey	DNQ
Hungary	Hungaroring	J. Palmer	DNF (engine)
		J. Bailey	DNQ
Belgium	Spa	J. Palmer	12
		J. Bailey	DNQ
Italy	Monza	J. Palmer	DNQ
		J. Bailey	12
Portugal	Estoril	J. Palmer	DNF (engine overheating)
		J. Bailey	DNQ
Spain	Jerez	J. Palmer	DNF (radiator)
		J. Bailey	DNQ
Japan	Suzuka	J. Palmer	12
		J. Bailey	14
Australia	Adelaide	J. Palmer	DNF (crown wheel)
		J. Bailey	DNQ

Championship: Senna (McLaren) 90; Prost (McLaren) 87;
G. Berger (Ferrari) 41; Palmer 5 (13th); Bailey 0.
Constructors': McLaren 199; Ferrari 65; Benetton 39; Tyrrell 5 (8th).

1989 (Tyrrell-Ford)

Brazil	Jacarepagua	J. Palmer	7
		M. Alboreto	10
San Marino	Imola	J. Palmer	6
		M. Alboreto	DNQ
Monaco	Monte Carlo	J. Palmer	9
		M. Alboreto	5
Mexico	Mexico City	J. Palmer	DNF (throttle)
		M. Alboreto	3

USA	Phoenix	J. Palmer	9
		M. Alboreto	DNF (gearbox)
Canada	Montreal	J. Palmer	DNF (crash)
		M. Alboreto	DNF (electrics)
France	Ricard	J. Palmer	10
		J. Alesi	4
Great Britain	Silverstone	J. Palmer	DNF (spin)
		J. Alesi	DNF (spin)
Germany	Hockenheim	J. Palmer	DNF (throttle)
		J. Alesi	10
Hungary	Hungaroring	J. Palmer	13
		J. Alesi	9
Belgium	Spa	J. Palmer	14
		J. Herbert	DNF (spin)
Italy	Monza	J. Palmer	DNF (engine)
		J. Alesi	5
Portugal	Estoril	J. Palmer	6
		J. Herbert	DNQ
Spain	Jerez	J. Palmer	10
		J. Alesi	4
Japan	Suzuka	J. Palmer	DNF (fuel leak)
		J. Alesi	DNF (gearbox)
Australia	Adelaide	J. Palmer	DNQ
		J. Alesi	DNF (electrics)

Championship: Prost (McLaren) 76; Senna (McLaren) 60; R. Patrese (Williams) 40; Alesi 8 (9th); Palmer 2 (23rd).
Constructors': McLaren 141; Williams 77; Ferrari 59; Tyrrell 16 (5th).

1990 (Tyrrell-Ford)

USA	Phoenix	S. Nakajima	6
		J. Alesi	2
Brazil	Interlagos	S. Nakajima	8
		J. Alesi	7
San Marino	Imola	S. Nakajima	DNF (crash)
		J. Alesi	6
Monaco	Monte Carlo	S. Nakajima	DNF (spin)
		J. Alesi	2
Canada	Montreal	S. Nakajima	11
		J. Alesi	DNF (crash)
Mexico	Mexico City	S. Nakajima	DNF (crash)
		J. Alesi	7
France	Ricard	S. Nakajima	DNF (gear linkage)
		J. Alesi	DNF (differential)
Great Britain	Silverstone	S. Nakajima	DNF (electrics)
		J. Alesi	8
Germany	Hockenheim	S. Nakajima	DNF (electrics)
		J. Alesi	11
Hungary	Hungaroring	S. Nakajima	DNF (spin)
		J. Alesi	DNF (crash)
Belgium	Spa	S. Nakajima	DNF (engine)
		J. Alesi	8
Italy	Monza	S. Nakajima	6
		J. Alesi	DNF (spin)
Portugal	Estoril	S. Nakajima	WITHDREW
		J. Alesi	8
Spain	Jerez	S. Nakajima	DNF (spin)
		J. Alesi	DNF (puncture - crash)

Japan	Suzuka	S. Nakajima	6
		J. Alesi	WITHDREW
Australia	Adelaide	S. Nakajima	DNF (spin)
		J. Alesi	8

Championship: Senna (McLaren) 78; Prost (Ferrari) 71; Piquet (Benetton) 43; Alesi 13 (9th); Nakajima 3 (14th).
Constructors': McLaren 121; Ferrari 110; Benetton 71; Tyrrell 16 (5th).

1991 (Tyrrell-Honda)

USA	Phoenix	S. Nakajima	5
		S. Modena	4
Brazil	Interlagos	S. Nakajima	DNF (spin)
		S. Modena	DNF (gearshift)
San Marino	Imola	S. Nakajima	DNF (transmission)
		S. Modena	DNF (transmission)
Monaco	Monte Carlo	S. Nakajima	DNF (spin)
		S. Modena	DNF (engine)
Canada	Montreal	S. Nakajima	10
		S. Modena	2
Mexico	Mexico City	S. Nakajima	12
		S. Modena	11
France	Magny-Cours	S. Nakajima	DNF (spin)
		S. Modena	DNF (gearbox)
Great Britain	Silverstone	S. Nakajima	8
		S. Modena	7
Germany	Hockenheim	S. Nakajima	DNF (gearbox)
		S. Modena	13
Hungary	Hungaroring	S. Nakajima	15
		S. Modena	12
Belgium	Spa	S. Nakajima	DNF (went off)
		S. Modena	DNF (oil leak)
Italy	Monza	S. Nakajima	DNF (throttle)
		S. Modena	DNF (engine)
Portugal	Estoril	S. Nakajima	13
		S. Modena	DNF (engine)
Spain	Catalunya	S. Nakajima	17
		S. Modena	16
Japan	Suzuka	S. Nakajima	DNF (suspension)
		S. Modena	6
Australia	Adelaide	S. Nakajima	DNF (crash)
		S. Modena	10

Championship: Senna (McLaren) 96; Mansell (Williams) 72; Patrese (Williams) 53; Modena 10 (8th); Nakajima 2 (15th).
Constructors': McLaren 139; Williams 125; Ferrari 55.5; Tyrrell 12 (6th).

1992 (Tyrrell-Ilmor)

South Africa	Kyalami	O. Grouillard	DNF (clutch)
		A. de Cesaris	DNF (engine)
Mexico	Mexico City	O. Grouillard	DNF (engine)
		A. de Cesaris	5
Brazil	Interlagos	O. Grouillard	DNF (engine)
		A. de Cesaris	DNF (electrics)
Spain	Catalunya	O. Grouillard	DNF (spin)
		A. de Cesaris	DNF (oil pressure)
San Marino	Imola	O. Grouillard	8
		A. de Cesaris	14

Monaco	Monte Carlo	O. Grouillard	DNF (gearbox)
		A. de Cesaris	DNF (gearbox)
Canada	Montreal	O. Grouillard	12
		A. de Cesaris	5
France	Magny-Cours	O. Grouillard	11
		A. de Cesaris	DNF (spin)
Great Britain	Silverstone	O. Grouillard	11
		A. de Cesaris	DNF (suspension)
Germany	Hockenheim	O. Grouillard	DNF (overheating)
		A. de Cesaris	DNF (engine)
Hungary	Hungaroring	O. Grouillard	DNF (crash)
		A. de Cesaris	8
Belgium	Spa	O. Grouillard	DNF (spin)
		A. de Cesaris	8
Italy	Monza	O. Grouillard	DNF (engine)
		A. de Cesaris	6
Portugal	Estoril	O. Grouillard	DNF (gearbox)
		A. de Cesaris	9
Japan	Suzuka	O. Grouillard	DNF (crash)
		A. de Cesaris	4
Australia	Adelaide	O. Grouillard	DNF (crash)
		A. de Cesaris	DNF (fuel pressure)

Championship: Mansell (Williams) 108; Patrese (Williams) 56;
M. Schumacher (Benetton) 53; De Cesaris 8 (9th); Grouillard 0.
Constructors': Williams 164; McLaren 99; Benetton 91; Tyrrell 8 (6th).

1993 (Tyrrell-Yamaha)

South Africa	Kyalami	U. Katayama	DNF (transmission)
		A. de Cesaris	DNF (transmission)
Brazil	Interlagos	U. Katayama	DNF (crash)
		A. de Cesaris	DNF (electrics)
Europe	Donington	U. Katayama	DNF (clutch)
		A. de Cesaris	DNF (gearbox)
San Marino	Imola	U. Katyama	DNF (engine)
		A. de Cesaris	DNF (gearbox)
Spain	Catalunya	U. Katayama	DNF (spin)
		A. de Cesaris	DSQ
Monaco	Monte Carlo	U. Katayama	DNF (oil leak)
		A. de Cesaris	10
Canada	Montreal	U. Katayama	17
		A. de Cesaris	DNF (crash)
France	Magny-Cours	U. Katayama	DNF (sump)
		A. de Cesaris	15
Great Britain	Silverstone	U. Katayama	13
		A de Cesaris	NC
Germany	Hockenheim	U. Katayama	DNF (transmission)
		A. de Cesaris	DNF (gearbox)
Hungary	Hungaroring	U. Katayama	10
		A. de Cesaris	11
Belgium	Spa	U. Katayama	15
		A. de Cesaris	DNF (engine)
Italy	Monza	U. Katayama	14
		A de Cesaris	13
Portugal	Estoril	U. Katayama	DNF (crash)
		A. de Cesaris	12
Japan	Suzuka	U. Katayama	DNF (engine)
		A. de Cesaris	DNF (crash)

(Schlegelmilch)

Australia	Adelaide	U. Katayama	DNF (crash)
		A. de Cesaris	13

Championship: Prost (Williams) 99; Senna (McLaren) 73;
D. Hill (Williams) 69; Katayama 0; de Cesaris 0.
Constructors': Williams 168; McLaren 84; Benetton 72; Tyrrell 0.

1994 (Tyrrell-Yamaha)

Brazil	Interlagos	U. Katayama	5
		M. Blundell	DNF (crash)
Pacific	Aida	U. Katayama	DNF (engine)
		M. Blundell	DNF (crash)
San Marino	Imola	U. Katayama	5
		M. Blundell	9
Monaco	Monte Carlo	U. Katayama	DNF (gearbox)
		M. Blundell	DNF (engine)
Spain	Catalunya	U. Katayama	DNF (engine)
		M. Blundell	3
Canada	Montreal	U. Katayama	DNF (spin)
		M. Blundell	10
France	Magny-Cours	U. Katayama	DNF (spin)
		M. Blundell	10
Great Britain	Silverstone	U. Katayama	6
		M. Blundell	DNF (gearbox)
Germany	Hockenheim	U. Katayama	DNF (throttle)
		M. Blundell	DNF (crash)
Hungary	Hungaroring	U. Katayama	DNF (crash)
		M. Blundell	5
Belgium	Spa	U. Katayama	DNF (engine)
		M. Blundell	5
Italy	Monza	U. Katayama	DNF (crash)
		M. Blundell	DNF (crash)
Portugal	Estoril	U. Katayama	DNF (gearbox)
		M. Blundell	DNF (engine)
Europe	Jerez	U. Katayama	7
		M. Blundell	13
Japan	Suzuka	U. Katayama	DNF (crash)
		M. Blundell	DNF (engine)

Australia	Adelaide	U. Katayama	DNF (spin)
		M. Blundell	DNF (crash)

Championship: Schumacher (Benetton) 92; Hill (Williams) 91;
Berger (Ferrari) 41; Blundell 8 (12th); Katayama 5 (17th).
Constructors': Williams 118; Benetton 103; Ferrari 71; Tyrrell 13 (6th).

1995 (Tyrrell-Yamaha)

Brazil	Interlagos	U. Katayama	DNF (spin)
		M. Salo	7
Argentina	Buenos Aires	U. Katayama	8
		M. Salo	DNF (crash)
San Marino	Imola	U. Katayama	DNF (spin)
		M. Salo	DNF (engine)
Spain	Catalunya	U. Katayama	DNF (engine)
		M. Salo	10
Monaco	Monte Carlo	U. Katayama	DNF (crash)
		M. Salo	DNF (engine)
Canada	Montreal	U. Katayama	DNF (engine)
		M. Salo	7
France	Magny-Cours	U. Katayama	DNF (crash)
		M. Salo	15
Great Britain	Silverstone	U. Katayama	DNF (fuel pressure)
		M. Salo	8
Germany	Hockenheim	U. Katayama	7
		M. Salo	DNF (clutch)
Hungary	Hungaroring	U. Katayama	DNF (crash)
		M. Salo	DNF (throttle)
Belgium	Spa	U. Katayama	DNF (spin)
		M. Salo	8
Italy	Monza	U. Katayama	10
		M. Salo	5
Portugal	Estoril	U. Katayama	DNS
		M. Salo	13
Europe	Nürburgring	G. Tarquini	14
		M. Salo	10
Pacific	Aida	U. Katayama	14
		M. Salo	12
Japan	Suzuka	U. Katayama	DNF (spin)
		M. Salo	6
Australia	Adelaide	U. Katayama	DNF (engine)
		M. Salo	5

Championship: Schumacher (Benetton) 102; Hill 69;
D. Coulthard (Williams) 49; Salo 5 (14th); Katayama 0; Tarquini 0.
Constructors': Benetton 137; Williams 112; Ferrari 73; Tyrrell 5 (8th).

1996 (Tyrrell-Yamaha)

Australia	Melbourne	U. Katayama	11
		M. Salo	6
Brazil	Interlagos	U. Katayama	9
		M. Salo	5
Argentina	Buenos Aires	U. Katayama	DNF (transmission)
		M. Salo	DNF (throttle)
Europe	Nürburgring	U. Katayama	DSQ
		M. Salo	DSQ
San Marino	Imola	U. Katayama	DNF (transmission)
		M. Salo	DNF (engine)
Monaco	Monte Carlo	U. Katayama	DNF (crash)
		M. Salo	5
Spain	Catalunya	U. Katayama	DNF (electrics)
		M. Salo	DSQ
Canada	Montreal	U. Katayama	DNF (crash)
		M. Salo	DNF (engine)
France	Magny-Cours	U. Katayama	DNF (engine)
		M. Salo	10
Great Britain	Silverstone	U. Katayama	DNF (engine)
		M. Salo	7
Germany	Hockenheim	U. Katayama	DNF (spin)
		M. Salo	9
Hungary	Hungaroring	U. Katayama	7
		M. Salo	DNF (crash)
Belgium	Spa	U. Katayama	8
		M. Salo	7
Italy	Monza	U. Katayama	10
		M. Salo	DNF (engine)
Portugal	Estoril	U. Katayama	12
		M. Salo	11
Japan	Suzuka	U. Katayama	DNF (engine)
		M. Salo	DNF (engine)

Championship: Hill (Williams) 97; J. Villeneuve (Williams) 78;
Schumacher (Ferrari) 59; Salo 5 (13th); Katayama 0.
Constructors': Williams 175; Ferrari 70; Benetton 68; Tyrrell 5 (8th).

1997 (Tyrrell-Ford)

Australia	Melbourne	J. Verstappen	DNF (crash)
		M. Salo	DNF (engine)
Brazil	Interlagos	J. Verstappen	15
		M. Salo	13
Argentina	Buenos Aires	J. Verstappen	DNF (fuel pressure)
		M. Salo	8
San Marino	Imola	J. Verstappen	10
		M. Salo	9
Monaco	Monte Carlo	J. Verstappen	8
		M. Salo	5
Spain	Catalunya	J. Verstappen	11
		M. Salo	DNF (puncture)
Canada	Montreal	J. Verstappen	DNF (air valve)
		M. Salo	DNF (engine)
France	Magny-Cours	J. Verstappen	DNF (throttle)
		M. Salo	DNF (engine)
Great Britain	Silverstone	J. Verstappen	DNF (engine)
		M. Salo	DNF (engine)
Germany	Hockenheim	J. Verstappen	10
		M. Salo	DNF (clutch)
Hungary	Hungaroring	J. Verstappen	DNF (pneumatic leak)
		M. Salo	13
Belgium	Spa	J. Verstappen	DNF (spin)
		M. Salo	11
Italy	Monza	J. Verstappen	DNF (engine)
		M. Salo	DNF (engine)
Austria	A1-Ring	J. Verstappen	12
		M. Salo	DNF (transmission)
Luxemburg	Nürburgring	J. Verstappen	DNF (engine)
		M. Salo	10

Japan	Suzuka	J. Verstappen	13
		M. Salo	DNF (engine)
Europe	Jerez	J. Verstappen	16
		M. Salo	12

Championship: Villeneuve (Williams) 81; H. Frentzen (Williams) 42;
Coulthard (McLaren), Alesi (Benetton) 36; Salo 2 (16th); Verstappen 0.
Constructors': Williams 123; Ferrari 102; Benetton 67; Tyrrell 2 (10th).

1998 (Tyrrell-Ford)

Australia	Melbourne	R. Rosset	DNF (gearbox)
		T. Takagi	DNF (crash)
Brazil	Interlagos	R. Rosset	DNF (gearbox)
		T. Takagi	DNF (engine)
Argentina	Buenos Aires	R. Rosset	14
		T. Takagi	12
San Marino	Imola	R. Rosset	DNF (engine)
		T. Takagi	DNF (engine)
Spain	Catalunya	R. Rosset	DNQ
		T. Takagi	13
Monaco	Monte Carlo	R. Rosset	DNQ
		T. Takagi	11
Canada	Montreal	R. Rosset	8
		T. Takagi	DNF (transmission)
France	Magny-Cours	R. Rosset	DNF (engine)
		T. Takagi	DNF (engine)
Great Britain	Silverstone	R. Rosset	DNF (spin)
		T. Takagi	9
Austria	A1-Ring	R. Rosset	12
		T. Takagi	DNF (crash)
Germany	Hockenheim	R. Rosset	DNQ
		T. Takagi	13
Hungary	Hungaroring	R. Rosset	DNQ
		T. Takagi	14
Belgium	Spa	R. Rosset	DNS
		T. Takagi	DNF (spin)
Italy	Monza	R. Rosset	12
		T. Takagi	9
Luxemburg	Nürburgring	R. Rosset	DNF (engine)
		T. Takagi	16
Japan	Suzuka	R. Rosset	DNQ
		T. Takagi	DNF (crash)

Championship: M. Häkkinen (McLaren) 100; Schumacher (Ferrari) 86;
Coulthard (McLaren) 56; Rosset 0; Takagi 0.
Constructors': McLaren 156; Ferrari 133; Williams 38; Tyrrell 0.

(Schlegelmilch)

Bibliography

Blunsden, John and Brinton, Alan *Motor Racing Year 1961* (Knightsbridge
   Group of Publications Limited, 1961).
Blunsden, John *Formula Junior* (Motor Racing Publications, 1961).
Carrick, Peter *Great Motor-Cycle Riders* (Hale, 1985).
Depailler, Patrick *La course est un conbat* (Calmann-Lévy, Paris, José
   Rosinski).
Deschenaux, Jacques *Marlboro Grand Prix Guide 2001* (Marlboro).
Donaldson, Gerald *Grand Prix People* (MRP, 1990)
   - *Villeneuve* (MRP, 1989).
Gauld Graham *Ecurie Ecosse* (Graham Gauld Public Relations Ltd, 1992).
Gill, Barrie *The Facts about a Grand Prix Team Featuring Elf Team
   Tyrrell* (G. Whizzard/André Deutsch, 1977).
Hallé, Jean-Claude *François Cevert 'la mort dans mon contrat'* (Éditions
   J'ai Lu, Paris, © Flammarion, 1974).
Hayhoe, David and Holland, David *The Grand Prix Data Book 1997*
   (Duke, 1996).
Hamilton, Maurice *Kimberley's Grand Prix Team Guide No. 7*, Tyrrell
   (Kimberley's, 1983).
Higham, Peter *The Guinness Guide to International Motor Racing*
   (Guinness Publishing, 1995).

Laborderie, Renaud de *François Cevert* (Solar, Paris, 1973).
Lang, Mike *Grand Prix!* (Volumes 1, 2 and 3) (Haynes).
McIntyre, Bob *Motor Cycling Today* (Arthur Barker Limited, 1962).
Petersens, Fredrik *The Viking Drivers* William Kimber, 1979).
Pomeroy, Laurence and Walkerley, Rodney *The Motor Year Book 1954*
   (Temple Press Limited).
Sheldon, Paul and Rabagliati *A Record of Grand Prix and Voiturette
   Racing Vol 6 1954-1959* (1987).
   - *Formula 1 Register Fact Book – Formula 3 1947-1952.*
   - *Formula 1 Register Fact Book – Formula 3 1953-1955.*
   - *Formula 1 Register Fact Book – Formula 3 1956-1962.*
*Shell International Petroleum Company Motorsport profiles No. 7 Ken
   Tyrrell* (Shell International.
Small, Steve *The Grand Prix Who's Who* (Guinness Publishing, 1996).
Stewart, Jackie and Dymock, Eric *World Champion* (Pelham Books,
   1970).
Stewart, Jackie and Manso, Peter *Faster!* (William Kimber, 1972)
Surtees, John *World Champion* (Edited by Alan Henry/ Hazleton
   Publishing, 1991).

INDEX